Kettingham

Ketteringham

A Norfolk Country Estate

Robert Sharpe

POPPYLAND
PUBLISHING

ℬ *To Leasa* ℭ

Picture credits:

Ancient House, 101
archive.org, 83*
Author's collection, 18, 38, 39, 41, 42, 47, 53, 55, 60, 67 (bottom), 77 (bottom), 100, 107, 109, 114, 137, 138, 139, 140
Folger Shakespeare Library, 57*
Garlick, M., 10*
Leggett, T., 117
Library of Congress, 30*, 103*
Mike Page collection, front cover, 123
National Galleries of Scotland, 85
National Maritime Museum, Greenwich, London, 68
Newsquest/Archant, 120
Norfolk County Council Library and Information Service, 89, 111
Poppyland Ltd collection, frontispiece, vi, 16, 34, 45, 46, 59, 74, 86, 119, 119, 126, 128
Thower, C., 50
University of Edinburgh, 25*
Wellcome collection, 26*, 76*, 87*
Westminster Abbey, 67 (top)
Unknown, 77 (top)
* under Creative Commons licence (CC BY-SA 2.0) or public domain.

Front Cover: Kettingham Hall, lake and church, 2008.
Frontispiece: Ketteringham Hall, 2006.

Contents

Abbreviations

NHER	Norfolk Historic Environmental Record.
NRO	Norfolk Record Office.
TNA	The National Archives.

16th and 17th century stained glass in the window of the main staircase at Ketteringham Hall.

Installed by Sir John Boileau in 1844, the central panel depicts 'Christus Bonus Pator' (Christ the Good Shepherd) and shows a shepherd with his crook and a sheep on his shoulder, and next to him on the ground are several pieces of discarded armour and weapons and a crown. This would seem to be an allegorical depiction of Emperor Charles V (1500–1558) who had retired in 1557 to live in a Spanish monastery.

Preface

Following an offer of a position as a design draughtsman at Lotus Cars at Hethel I began looking for a house. I do not believe in paying to go to work, so it had to be within cycling distance. There was a property for sale in Ketteringham and I bought it. In a straight line it was only one and a half miles from Lotus. The cycle ride was, however, nearly four. It was a very pleasant journey along narrow country roads with very little traffic. Although only four road were involved, they differed in character. The first two were straight crossing large open fields whereas the last two meandered between smaller, hedged fields. Why the difference, never crossed my mind. Five years later it did not matter as due to a downturn in the economy I, along with many others, was made redundant.

I became a contract automotive design engineer. I worked on many projects in various countries keeping my home in Ketteringham. While on a Far-East contract, my wife became pregnant and we returned to Ketteringham. I decided I would be a full-time Dad. To keep 'the brain ticking over' I enrolled with the Open University and began a history degree. Soon after our return to Ketteringham a local parish councillor, Ingid Fairman, invited anyone interested in forming a village history group to attend a meeting at the village hall. I joined the group and became treasurer. As the depth of the village history became apparent, I realised it needed to be recorded. With great naivety I decided to write a book on the history of Ketteringham. The history group was turning up historic fact after historic fact but how to join these together to form a narrative? I completed the final module of my degree at the UEA in landscape archaeology. Those cycle rides to Lotus began to make sense. The landscape of open fields was once Ketteringham common. The reason the route was not direct was because it followed ancient field boundaries. To understand the village history I had to start with the landscape. It may appear obvious that the history of a rural community is all about the land, but this was only to be my starting point. Dr Mary Parker, the group secretary, uncovered fascinating information on the Boileau family who owned not only the Hall but the whole village. How was it that all the land in Ketteringham belonged to one family? I had a story to uncover.

This book could not have been written if it had not been for the Ketteringham and East Carleton History Group. It is now over eighteen years since it was formed. I wish to thank Ingrid Fairman, chairman, Dr Mary Parker, secretary and the small group of regulars who attend the monthly meetings at the village hall. I must also apologise that all the vast amount of history they have unearthed could not be included here. Having mentioned the importance of land regarding the village's history I am grateful to the landowners for allowing me access to their land. I described my naivety on starting this book. This is reflected in the time it has taken me to complete it. Time during which some of those who have helped are sadly no longer with us. I remember the help Catherine Hadingham, Joy Allen, George Evans, Dr Simon Hampton and Harry and Rachel Hornor gave me. Finally I wish to thank Sandra Howard and Dr Mary Parker for proof reading this work.

Robert Sharpe, 2023.

Introduction

An estate village is a village that exists within a private estate or put another way, that exists in an area of privately-owned land. The desire to own land has always been important to people—a small piece of land to build a family dwelling or a larger piece to produce enough food for the family. Additional land provides the possibility for generating a surplus of food which can then be sold for profit. Larger land holdings can be rented to tenants for greater income. Income becomes wealth. Wealth generally leads to an increase in status and ultimately power. The acquisition of land has therefore not surprisingly been the desire of many throughout time.

The small area of Norfolk we now call Ketteringham has evidence of land ownership going back 4000 years. This takes the form of two large mounds of soil at the east end of Ketteringham High Street. These are Bronze Age burial mounds. Their size and location were designed to make a statement in the landscape. 'This is the land of our ancestors'. There were others that combine to mark out the communal land.[1] The community would take many forms as different groups arrived from the Continent. Of these it would be the Anglo-Saxons and Vikings who left the greatest legacy. It was their structure of land ownership that the Normans took over, following William's victory at Hastings in 1066. The Domesday survey which followed in 1086 records Saxon Kitrincham as having three manors. Two belonging to the Saxon Thegn Ulf and one to Ketil. These would be given to the Norman lords, Ulf's to Bigod and Ketil's to Peverel. Domesday records just over half the population as freemen or sokemen[2] during this time. They owned approximately half of the cultivated land. The cultivated land was divided equally between villagers and lords. The land of the villagers of Ketteringham provided a subsistence living. The Saxon Thegns and later Norman lords owned additional land elsewhere. The combined land holding generated wealth and, in turn, status.

Although Ketteringham is described as having three manors at the Domesday survey it was only the larger of Bigod's two manors that had its manorial hall in Ketteringham. The other two were only land holdings with their manor houses in other villagers. The manor house of Ketteringham was inhabited by the lord's representative and was consequentially likely not a particularly grand building at this time. With no one with any status living in Ketteringham, the village was of little significance beyond the income it gave the two lords. History tends not to record and therefore give any significance to the lowly folk who called it home and lived off the land.

In 1168 Ketteringham Hall manor passed to Aubrey de Vere, Earl of Oxford. The De Veres' family seat was Hedingham Castle and so they had little interest in living

Hedingham Castle keep, the De Vere's family seat.

at Ketteringham Hall. It did, however, become the home of Aubrey's daughter Julianne following her separation from Hugh Bigod. This was an important point in Ketteringham's history as the Hall was now the home of a member of an important family. The manor later became the home of Lora de Vere who married Sir Reginald Argentine in 1265, and the manor became known as Argentine's manor. The manor was sold to Sir William Appleyard. After his death, his widow Emma married Henry Grey in 1416 and the manor became the seat of the Greys. In 1495, Sir William Grey joined the second manor once owned by Bigod with Ketteringham Hall manor.

As the Medieval period ended, Ketteringham was the seat of an important family with a large landholding in Ketteringham.

Notes

1. Pryor, *The Making of the British Landscape*, p.97.
2. A freeman with certain obligations to the lord.

An Estate to Challenge the King

O n a cold day in late November 1677, a messenger left Wymondham on the
final leg of his journey from Windsor Castle. He rode across Ketteringham
common and arrived at his destination, Ketteringham Hall. The Tudor Hall was
the seat of the Heveningham family. He duly delivered the message for Lady Mary
Heveningham. Her husband, Sir William, had died.

As she came to terms with her loss, I am sure Lady Mary kept returning to that
October day eighteen years earlier when they came for her husband. On that
fateful day in 1660 he, and seventeen others, had been arrested and taken to the
Tower of London pending trial. All had been placed in solitary confinement with
no access to legal advice. They were only told of the charge they faced the night
before their trial. They were charged under the Treason Act of 1351. This was an
old piece of legislation introduced 300 years earlier in the reign of Edward III. It
defined treason as, "here a man doth compass or imagine the death of our said
Lord the King in his realm, or be adherent to the enemies of our Lord the King
in his realm, giving to them aid or support in his realm or elsewhere...". Even if
they had received the best legal advice in the land and greater time to consider
the charge, the breadth of this definition would have made planning any defence
very difficult. Sir William knew his past would make it near impossible. He had
supported Parliament in the Civil War against the King and, even worse, having
been appointed as a commissioner of the High Court of Justice; he had served at
the trial of Charles I[1]. He had been a regular participant during the trial of the King
and was there when the sentence was read out; the defendant "shall be put to death
by the severing of his head from his body". The only small grounds of hope he had
were that, when the death warrant was presented, of the 67 commissioners present
(at the sentencing) only 57 actually signed it. Sir William Heveningham was one
of the 10 who had not signed. Lady Mary was not sure why her husband had not
signed. Maybe there was insufficient room left on the document or perhaps to
execute his King was a step too far.[2]

The day following the signing of the death warrant, 30 January 1649, the King
was executed. England became a republic but in 1661 the monarchy had been
restored. Charles's son had returned from exile and now reigned as King Charles II
of England and he wanted revenge upon those who had participated in the death
of his father.

On the 8 October 1660, Sir William and the others were taken to Hicks Hall,
Clerkenwell, the session house of the county of Middlesex. The court was presided

Facsimile of Charles I death warrant, Sir William Hevingham did not sign it.

over by Bridgeman along with 10 other judges and 34 commissioners. At the court, Sir William Heveningham was one of the first groups of three brought to the bar and asked how they pleaded to the charge. The first prisoner, Sir Hardress Waller, despite attempts at clarification of the charge, was cornered into pleading guilty. Next, Thomas Harrison was not so easily manipulated and pleaded not guilty. Having watched as the other two's attempts at discussion failed, Sir William Heveningham gave a plea of not guilty. The remainder of the accused were in turn called to the bar and they too all pleaded not guilty.

During the trial Sir William and the others argued that they had been put under duress and were not fully aware of what they were involved in. That such learned and influential men had been forced to go along with the trial of the King with little knowledge of what was happening was, not surprisingly, dismissed by the jury who found them all guilty. Once guilt had been determined, the sentences were handed out. At this moment Sir William was asked to step aside from the bar. Judge Bridgeman appeared to have been given last minute instructions and was unsure as to what he should say. He was required to make some comment so told Sir William, "I presume some time will be given to him to consider something relating to him before any order will be given for his execution".[3] Sir William may have thought he was being singled out from the others for sentence because he had not actually signed the death warrant. Lady Mary knew it was as a result of the actions of her father, the wealthy and influential Earl of Dover. Whether her father had chosen to let his son-in-law sweat until the last minute before choosing to bring his influence to his son-in-law's aid, she did not know.[4] His co-accused were sentenced to death. Sir William had been saved from execution but was sentenced to life imprisonment in Windsor Castle.[5]

No doubt Lady Mary, coming to terms with the loss of her husband, requested a meeting with the vicar at St Peter's, Ketteringham, Robert Pecket. The church and vicarage were, as now, but a short walk from the Hall. Sir William had presented Robert Pecket to the living of Ketteringham in 1652[6] and he too would have remembered the day Sir William was arrested. If the King took the estate what would become of him? Life for a priest without a patron would be comparable to that of a landless labourer. He agreed to Lady Mary's request that her husband's body should be laid to rest in the church vault which she had built. When her time came to join Sir William this would be where she too was to be buried, in "the chambers of the Church of Ketteringham".[7] Ketteringham was to remain her family seat until her death in 1696.

Ketteringham is a small Norfolk village unknown to most in the county of Norfolk let alone the country at large. Even locally it is largely only known as it is the former site of a South Norfolk Council's Recycling Centre.[8] It is perhaps, therefore understandable to start a history of this small, little-known village, with the part it played in a major and familiar historical event. The English Civil War, with its resulting regicide, is clearly one of the major events of British history and, I would argue, world history. The rift between King and Parliament was not caused by Sir William Heveningham. His role in its eventual outcome was only minor and a far from decisive one. The reason for choosing this moment in history with relation to Ketteringham's story is that it is evidence of what Ketteringham had become. By the 17th century Ketteringham Hall was the family seat of a branch of the Heveningham family who were of sufficient status to be part of a successful challenge to the King of England, and the target of the revenge of the next. A grand residence or a title is not required to be part of a rebellion; many of those who lost their lives in the Civil War were of humble birth. The Civil War was initially a revolt by Parliamentarians at a time when to stand for Parliament required ownership of land. The Ketteringham estate fulfilled this requirement. Land by itself, however, was unlikely to enable one to enter the world of Parliament. This required contacts and support from the ruling elite. In order to socialise and be accepted in such circles a grand residence with a fine estate was a prerequisite. By the mid-17th century Ketteringham Hall had become such a residence. The Ketteringham estate was an asset that allowed Sir William Heveningham not only to socialise with the important families of England but to marry into this influential circle. His first wife had been Catherine, daughter of Sir Henry Wallop MP, an extremely wealthy and influential resident of Hampshire and Wiltshire. After her death Sir William married Mary, the daughter of the Earl of Dover who saved Sir William from execution.

When looking at a community's history there is often a point in the story when one particular aspect develops into the community's dominant and defining feature.

For some this may be the discovery of minerals in land nearby, which results in the community playing a particular role in events such as the Industrial Revolution. Another, might be, that its position on the coast makes it an ideal location for trading in new commodities or a gateway to new lands. In Ketteringham's case, the settlement had developed to become the seat of an influential family. This family lived at Ketteringham Hall surrounded by their estate which would become the entire village. Ketteringham's defining feature is as an estate village.

The new role of a settlement tends to come with an economic dimension which invariably leads to a growth in population turning a village into a town and possibly that town into a city. The importance of that one development can become the driving force of the settlement's history for centuries to come. Once the character of a place is defined, the loss of that characteristic or role can also become a definition, with towns and villages being described as 'former'. Communities are categorised as, for example, a former mining town or fishing village. This often takes the community's history in a new direction as it comes to terms with changing economic fortunes and searches for a new role for what has become a large population. Coming to terms with this is a major part of their more recent history. As an estate village with an economy based on agriculture, Ketteringham did not experience population growth. Once it ceased to be an estate village the economy remained largely agricultural and the population did not grow. Although no longer an estate village, its former heritage is still easily detected in the modern village.

All villages are special and have a history, a story, which should be told. Ketteringham is special in its estate village heritage but not unique in a rural county such as Norfolk. It is rare, however, in that the whole village was part of the estate but what makes it stand out is that it remained as such well into the 20th century. Ketteringham's evolution as an estate village is the narrative which drives the village's history and will flow through this book.

A village story needs a starting point. That might be when the first individuals settled in that area or when the settlement first took on a name. In the case of Ketteringham that would be either 10,000 years ago when a family of hunter gathers adopted a watering hole on the edge of the boulder clay plateau in an area now called Ketteringham or, when the Anglo-Saxon Cytra made this the location for his farmstead. Cytra-ingas-ham, farmstead (ham) belonging to (ingas) Cytra or Cytra's people. Although both starting points would create interesting journeys, they are both complex and long and therefore ones which can be travelled in another book. This chapter began with the Heveninghams established at Ketteringham. I will start this part of the journey with their arrival at Ketteringham Hall in 1496 when Thomas Heveningham, through his wife Anne, inherited Ketteringham Hall Manor from Sir Henry Grey. This was only 10 years after the Battle of Bosworth, an event historians generally consider to be the point which brought the medieval period to an end. This book therefore starts its story as the Medieval Period becomes the Early Modern Period and a new family moves into the manor house.

Notes

1. Walsh & Don, *The King's Revenge*, p.213-24.
2. Ibid., p.52-3.
3. Ibid., p.213-24.
4. Hunter believes Sir William was spared having surrendered on the proclamation of June 6 1660, *The History and Topography of Ketteringham in the County of Norfolk*, p.46.
5. Ibid.,1, p.213-24.
6. Blomefield, *An Essay Towards A Topographical History of the County of Norfolk*: vol.5, p.90.
7. TNA, Cat. Ref: Prob/11/433.
8. Prior to publication this closed in 2021.

St Peter's Church, 2004.

Thomas Heveningham inherits a Medieval Manor

On the death of Sir Henry Grey in 1496, Ketteringham Hall manor passed to Thomas Heveningham through his wife Anne.[1] Thomas Heveningham died only three years after inheriting the Manor and is buried, along with Anne, in the chancel of Ketteringham church. His choice of burial place is an important one. It indicates that Ketteringham was not only his home for his final few years but also the place he considered to be the family seat for his branch of the Heveningham family. This is a situation that would continue for the next two hundred years, the longest period for any family in Ketteringham's history.

I chose to describe Thomas Heveningham as inheriting the Ketteringham Hall Manor rather than Estate. In his will Sir Henry Grey bequeathed "My Manor of Ketteringham ... to Thomas Heveningham, and Anne, his wife".[2] The term manor originated in the medieval feudal system where tenants held land from the Lord for rent or service. The medieval term is an apt description as the Ketteringham

Chamber tomb in St. Peter's Church, Ketteringham.
The brass, centre left, depicts Thomas Heveningham and his five sons.

Manor they inherited was part of a largely medieval settlement. The reference to Hall in the name is a means of distinguishing it from the other two manors recorded in the Domesday Book 400 years earlier. Both of these were land holdings in Ketteringham[3] which belonged to manors whose main manor houses or halls were situated in other settlements. The medieval hall, that became Thomas and Anne's new home, would be replaced by later Heveninghams and that in turn modified to become the Victorian gothic Hall we see today. Although it is unlikely we will ever know much about the medieval hall, it is possible to gain an insight into wider medieval Ketteringham of which it was an important part. This is possible because the modern village layout is still remarkably similar to that of the medieval one. Many of the medieval ways that defined that layout define the structure of the modern village.

Despite modern Ketteringham having few roads, four converge at the eastern edge of the village to form a crossroads, now known as Ketteringham Five Ways. The reason they converge at this particular point is because of the two large mounds of earth located here, one sitting in the middle of the junction, the other just to the south. These mounds are tumuli, Bronze Age burial barrows which date back 4,000 years.[4] There was once a third burial mound 580 metres to the east of these. They mark a much older track that once connected the communities of the river estuary with those inland.[5] This track was later adopted by the Romans as part of their road network from their town, Venta Icenorum[6] near Caister St Edmund. Medieval villagers would have known this as the Intewda way, way to Intwood. Modern Cantley Lane they would have referred to as the Highway to Norwich. Ketteringham High Street would still be called the Gata from the Danish for street,

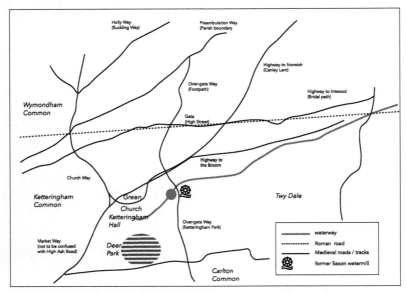

Medieval roads / tracks (modern names are in brackets).

a reminder that Ketteringham was once part of the Dane Law. The road that runs between Hethersett and East Carleton were constructed in the 19th century.

By the end of the 15th century, open field farming was no longer practiced in Ketteringham. This form of farming and land management had been in operation for hundreds of years and the layout of land reflected this. Many of the former system of open field administration would have remained. The Heveninghams, as Lords of the Manor, would have known the advantage that this afforded them. Open field farming had divided the arable land into three great fields known as, Cartuna fielde (Carlton Field), Hederseta fielde (Hethersett field) and Kitrincham fielde (Ketteringham field).[7] Within each field were strips of land of an acre in size. Each family owned a number of strips in each of the three fields. Since the 14th century, or possibly earlier, these strips had been exchanged or sold with neighbouring ones to create enclosures, what we would now refer to as fields. Evidence of the former strips can still be seen today in some of the irregular field boundaries. At the time of Thomas Heveningham, the enclosure may have been of a few strips creating a patchwork of small enclosures. The original large fields had paths providing access to the strips. One of the main paths crossing the Gata was known as Over Gata Waye. Today, to the south of High Street it is called Ketteringham Park, to the North it exists as a footpath. This path still has the reverse 'S' route formed by the need to manoeuvre a medieval eight ox plough.[8]

The Domesday book records the main manor as being taken from the Anglo-Saxon Thegn Ulf and given to the Norman Bigod after the Norman Conquest. From the information given, I estimate that this manor, which would become known as Ketteringham Hall manor, consisted of approximately 280 acres of arable land and 8 acres of meadow. This is supported by an inquest in 1382 following the death of Sir John Argentine.[9] (The Argentines had owned the manors before the Greys.) This would have been the size of the manor that passed to the Heveninghams, however, not long before he died Sir Henry Grey purchased the second largest manor in Ketteringham combining it with Ketteringham Hall manor.[10] This added a further 210 acres of arable and 4 more acres of meadow. At a time when land ownership inferred wealth and status, the increase in arable of 75% was significant.

Ketteringham is on the edge of the ridge of a boulder clay plateau that runs through the centre of Norfolk. The ridge is visible at Five Ways where it rises above the lower land of the Yare valley. An ideal place to make a statement in the landscape such as burial mounds. Here the soil is a light loam. As one travels west along the High Street (Gata) the ground becomes much heavier and at the west end of High Street it is heavy clay. Such land could not be ploughed with medieval farming technology. This was not a problem because this land still played an important role in the rural economy. It was an area where animals such as deer, hare and wildfowl could be hunted. Rabbits had not yet been introduced into Britain. Wild fruit, nuts, edible plants and honey could also be found. It supplied wood for burning and timber for building. This was referred to as the waste, a former name for common. That does not mean it was in common ownership. It belonged to Ketteringham Hall manor. The inhabitants of Ketteringham had used this land as a resource to supplement their arable lands for centuries, during which time, through custom and precedent, commoners right had evolved. As owners of the common, the Greys would have agreed what the commoners of Ketteringham could use the common for. These rights were strictly regulated with breaches of the rules tried in the leet court. Thomas Heveningham would have honoured these rights when he took possession.

Typically, the six main rights were: pasture (the grazing of cattle, sheep, ponies and horses), estovers (wood for the repair of buildings, fencing and for fuel), turbary (to cut turf and peat), piscary (to fish), pannage (release pigs into the woods to feed on acorns and beech mast) and locally common in the soil (to take gravel and clay from the common).

Ketteringham Common was part of a huge expanse of heavy land that separated Great Melton, Wymondham, Hethersett, Ashwellthorpe and Ketteringham. It was divided into local commons each belonging to a specific parish. The division between Ketteringham Common and Wymondham Common (known as Norwich Common) was marked by a medieval earthen bank which is still evident in places today.[11]

Kitrincham in the Late Saxon and Early Norman period was a nucleated settlement of wooden houses close to the church and its green. Ketteringham today has no church green and the only properties remaining near the church are the old vicarage, the rectorial house and Ketteringham Hall. Open field farming meant a family's landholding, either free or bonded, was located in different parts of the large open fields. They could not be close to all their land but the need to access the common as a resource was an important, constant requirement and justified relocation of their dwelling. The new dwellings were located on the Common edge where the end of the High Street (now called Low Street) joined Ketteringham Lane. The village had migrated here long before the Greys left the manor to the Heveninghams.

Thomas Heveningham was the largest landowner in the village, the second largest was the church. Ketteringham church had once belonged to Ketteringham Hall manor but had been appropriated by Pentney Priory. Under common law, the Church and its revenue were viewed as units of property that could be bought and exchanged by individuals or persons corporate such as abbeys and monastic houses. This process is known as appropriation and occurred in 37% of the parishes of Norfolk including Ketteringham.[12]

Robert de Vaux had founded Pentney Priory in 1140 while in charge of Ketteringham Hall manor.[13] At a similar time, St Peter's church was appropriated to Pentney Priory. Appropriation meant the Prior of Pentney took over the living of St Peter's as rector. He then appointed a resident priest or vicar. The appropriation of Ketteringham church was of financial benefit to the Priory but at the expense of the parish. The Priory took the great tithes, that is 10% of the crops grown in Ketteringham. These were originally intended to support the priest in his work, but he was left with the much smaller income provided from some glebe land and fees paid when he under took his religious duties. The glebe land belonging to the vicar was 28 acres but the Priory had 52 acres.[14]

As rector, the Prior built a dwelling for his representatives and a second smaller one for his resident priest. Blomefield describes the rectory as being "worth 10 marks at first,

The font, St Peter's Church Ketteringham.

after at 15 marks", whereas the vicarage was only worth 5 marks.[15] It is assumed the term "first" and "after" is reference to before and after the Reformation i.e., 1540s. Clearly the rectory by this time was worth at least twice that of the vicarage and it is likely to have been similar in earlier times.

The earliest church was likely a small wooden structure constructed for the Anglo-Saxon Thegn. This was later replaced by a flint structure. Having paid for these buildings the Thegn felt that implied ownership. It is questionable whether later owners of the manor also owned the church. This did not stop those who owned the Hall assuming that the church, so conveniently built next to their Hall, was their private chapel. Although the Greys did not own it, they appear to have been happy to pay for its upkeep and to adorn the interior with items that implied it was theirs and reflected their status. Sir Henry Grey's father, also Henry, and mother Emma paid for a new roof and windows for the chancel.[16]

Blomefield states that in the 15th century Henry Grey and his wife Emma rebuilt the chancel.[17] This, however, was more likely a remodelling of the 13th century rebuild[18]. It did include new windows and a new roof. The amount and type of work the Greys carried out on the church may be uncertain but they have left clear evidence of their close association with St Peter's. In the main panel of the east window, Sir Henry Grey is depicted in full armour. At the top of the panels, four shields display his ancestry including that of John de Mowbray, the second Duke, who died in 1432. He was the nephew of Sir Henry's mother and it may have been a memorial to him in 1435. The Greys chose St Peter's as their resting place and brasses of both Sir Henry and Jane Grey are now placed on the south wall of the chancel.[19] The brass to Sir Henry is now lost. The oldest bell in St Peter's belfry is from 1420 when the Greys would have been patron. The font also displays a connection with the Greys with the coats of arms of Heveninghams and Redisham carved on the base.[20]

The Grey family invested in the church and probably saved it from ruin. They saw Ketteringham Hall as the family seat and it is therefore likely they also invested in the Hall. We do not know what Ketteringham Hall was like at the time. It was not the Victorian gothic Hall we see today or the one that stood before that. The building was, I suspect, in reasonable condition. Although only at Ketteringham for 80 years, the Greys left their mark on the village's history. The manor Thomas and Anne Heveningham inherited was a modest but desirable medieval manor upon which they, and their descendants, could also leave their mark.

Notes

1. Hunter, *The History and Topography of Ketteringham in the county of Norfolk*, p.39.
2. Ibid., p.38.
3. At the time it was known as Kitrincham.
4. Historic England, entry: 1002888.
5. Sharpe, *The Journal of the Open University History Society*, p.16-21.
6. Venta Icenorum was a Roman town built after the Boudica rebellion of AD60.
7. NRO Glebe terriers 1635 DN/TER 93/1/1-33.
8. Rackham, *The History of the Countryside: The classic history of Britain's landscape, flora and fauna*, p.167-72.
9. Ibid.1, p.24.
10. Blomefield, *An Essay Towards A Topographical History of the County of Norfolk*: vol.5, p.96.
11. Norfolk Explorer, NHER No 22596.
12. Wade-Martins ed., *An Historical Atlas of Norfolk*, p.62.
13. Ibid. 9, p.89.
14. Ibid.
15. Ibid.
16. Ibid., p.92.
17. Ibid.
18. Rose, 9515 Ketteringham.
19. Sir Francis Boileau refers to a tomb on the floor of the Chancel which may have been the Greys. NRO PD42/12.
20. Ibid. 9, p.95.

The Heveninghams' Quest for Status

Much of the history of the village is intertwined with the history of the families who lived at Ketteringham Hall. Their fortunes, good or bad, have been felt by all who dwelt in the village. The story of how the Heveningham family gained influence and status is important to the village's history. A family's status can be seen by the grandeur and setting of the family's home. Ketteringham Hall and its grounds would be developed accordingly. Before considering how the rise in status was reflected in the Hall, its grounds and the village it is first necessary to consider how the Heveninghams went about achieving such status and standing.

Sir John Boileau, who purchased the Ketteringham Estate in 1837, commissioned Joseph Hunter to write a history of Ketteringham. In this work he describes Sir John Heveningham, who inherited the Hall from his father Thomas, as, "holding the offices usually filled by the county gentlemen of the better class".[1] This is likely in connection with Sir John Heveningham becoming Sheriff of Norfolk and Suffolk in 1508 and 1524. Such a position tended to be offered to established landed gentry with a certain standing or, alternatively, one not of 'better class' but having contacts. The latter may be case with Sir John as he took over the role of Sheriff from Sir John Shelton.

Sir John Heveningham married Alice, the daughter of Sir Ralph Shelton, in 1481.[2] Marriage was seen as a means of 'bettering' oneself and the Heveninghams made a good choice when they married into the Shelton family. Sir John Shelton's second wife was the daughter of Sir William Boleyn of Blickling Hall, Norfolk. When Henry VIII chose Ann Boleyn for his second wife Sir John became uncle to the Queen of England. Sir John and Lady Shelton became Governor and Governess to Princess Elizabeth, the future Queen Elizabeth I.

Sir John Heveningham died in 1536 and Ketteringham Hall passed to his son Anthony Heveningham. He married Katherine, the daughter of Sir Philip Calthorpe, and they had a son Henry. Katherine died in 1546 and Sir Anthony, like his father, then married into the Shelton family, marrying the daughter of Sir John Shelton, Mary. When Anthony died in 1557, he was buried in a tomb in the north side of Ketteringham church chancel. Although it is now lost, it is known to have been adorned with the arms of Heveningham combined with those of Shelton.

The importance of marriage as a way of 'bettering' oneself is clear. Evidence of the wish to promote the desirability of a daughter for this purpose can be seen at an inquest following Sir Anthony's death. A covenant had been made between Sir Anthony and Edmund Windham, of Felbrigg Hall, that Sir Anthony's son and heir Henry should marry one of his daughters, either Anne or Jane and gave Sir Anthony £266 13s 4d as a marriage portion. He was to marry Anne but had no children with her or his second wife, Anne daughter of Eden of Sudbury.[3] It is interesting that a father would pay a large amount to see his daughter married even to a family not of the county's 'better class'.

Along with marriage, the ownership of land was very important. Henry increased the holding of Ketteringham Hall manor with the purchase of part of Kangham's manor, the remainder going to Stanfield Hall. This was the final tidying up of the last remains of the complex Anglo-Saxon manorial system and, in so doing, made Ketteringham Hall the sole manor. The addition of these manorial lands can be seen by the square of land that protrudes from Ketteringham's southern parish boundary. The boundary runs through Stanfield Hall where it is possible to spend the night in either Ketteringham or Wymondham.

As Henry Heveningham had no children on his death his half-brother, Sir Arthur Heveningham, inherited the Hall in 1574. In addition to Ketteringham, he also owned: Fretenham, Gissing, Shropham and South-Walsham in Norfolk; Heveningham, Ubestone, Walpole, Cookeley, and Stibton in Suffolk; and Goldhanger in Essex.[4] It was, however, Ketteringham Hall which he considered his home and the family seat.

Arthur appears to have decided he was going to make a name for himself. In 1571 he was appointed to the Norfolk bench, in 1581and 1602 he was Sheriff of Norfolk and in 1588 he became Deputy Lieutenant of the county.[5] His father and grandfather had been content to marry into local Norfolk families, but he chose Mary Hanchet from Hertfordshire. They had thirteen children but only two, his eldest son, John and one of the younger daughters Abigail, married county families. John's second wife was Bridget, daughter of Christopher Paston and Abigail married Augustine Pettus, from a Norwich Aldermanic family. At a time when marriages were arranged by families for the benefit of the two families this would suggest that, despite the Heveningham's perceived wealth, they were not a popular Norfolk family.

Although not popular, Sir Arthur was an important member of an influential group within the county. A fellow member was Sir Edward Clere of Ormesby and Blickling who owned more property in the county than anyone apart from the Duke of Norfolk. He, like Sir Arthur, was also not popular. Their group, including William Heydon, John Peyton and Robert Buxton held the view that local administration should implement policies formulated by central government. The other group in Norfolk consisting of Nathaniel and Nicolas Bacon, Henry Gawdy, Francis Wyndham and William Blennerhassett put county interests first, these being the interests of the landowners. It is not surprising that Sir Arthur was not popular with many of his fellow county gentry.[6] His active interest in county politics is likely to have resulted in meetings taking place at the groups country houses. This would have included Ketteringham Hall which would need to be as grand as the other group member's houses.

Sir Arthur Heveningham's desire to gain standing and influence included becoming a Member of Parliament. In 1603, King James Stuart become James I of England and James VI of Scotland. Many, including, the Heveninghams, expected Parliament to meet at this time and Sir Arthur saw it as his opportunity to stand for Parliament. He was at that time, however, Sheriff of Norfolk and therefore not able to stand [7] so he decided to support his son John's bid. He wrote to Sir Thomas Knvyett of Ashwellthorpe

Engraving of James I by G. B. Shaw after the original at the Palace of Holyroodhouse.

suggesting that Sir Thomas's son, also Thomas, should stand with John for the county seats. Hoping to influence the vote, he suggested he might assist them by moving the hustings (a county court which he, as Sheriff, sat on) to a location in south Norfolk which would favour their sons while disadvantaging their rivals, Bacon and Gawdy. The expected Parliament was not, however, called until 1604 by which time Sir Arthur was free to stand. This he did but was defeated most likely due to his tendency to upset people. Sir Arthur never became a Member of Parliament.

Sir Arthur Heveningham's near obsession with obtaining and maintaining influence played its part in the selection of his son John's wives. John was married to Katherine, daughter of Lord Mordaunt. When she died in 1602, he married Bridget daughter of Christopher, son of Sir Christopher Paston. (She is buried in the chancel with the arms of Heveningham impaling Paston.)[8] John was knighted in 1603 and, like his father, took on many influential positions, becoming Justice of Peace for Norfolk 1608-22, then Suffolk from 1622 until his death. He was also Sheriff of Norfolk from 1615-16.[9]

In 1625 James I died and his son Charles became King. Unlike his father, Charles was not one for compromise and flexibility in political matters. This attitude led to England becoming involved with wars, firstly with Spain and then with both France and Spain. The financial and military requirements resulting from these conflicts caused Charles to use his emergency 'prerogative' powers, which in turn resulted in Parliament fearing a move toward royal 'absolutism'. Many books have been written on the English Civil War which can supply great detail and insight on this complex episode of history. Here, I will only concentrate on those in which the Heveninghams were involved.

During the conflict with France, Charles's favourite, the Duke of Buckingham, George Villiers, led a military expedition to help the French Huguenots (Calvinist Protestants) besieged by French troops at La Rochelle. This turned into a fiasco resulting in Parliament starting impeachment procedure against Buckingham. The only

George Villiers, Duke of Buckingham.

way the King could protect his favourite was to dissolve Parliament. The King still needed to pay for his war so he ordered an enforced loan equivalent of five subsidies. This did indeed raise money, £240,000, but caused resentment with many who considered it a means of taxation without the agreement of Parliament. Seventy-six gentlemen and the Earl of Lincoln were imprisoned for their refusal to pay this enforced loan. This included both John Heveningham and his son William, although William did not go to prison. Five of the gentlemen took out a writ of habeas corpus against their imprisonment, these were Sir William Coryton, Sir Thomas Darnell, Sir Walter Earle and Sir John Heveningham. At the trial Sir John was represented by serjeant John Bramston, who argued that under Magna Carta, "no man should be imprisoned but by the legal judgement of his peers or by *lex terrae*". The judges did not rule in their favour and the men were required to spend further time in prison.[10]

The verdict of the King's Bench judges was that the King had the right in this particular case to imprison the five who refused to pay the loan. The King however, declared that a King had the right to imprison people without any cause other than 'reasons of state'. Charles had allowed the attorney general, Sir Robert Heath, to falsify the legal recordings to uphold the right of a King to imprison without trial. When Members of Parliament learnt of this they were none too pleased. The MPs were united in preventing the King being able to carry out such acts again and Charles had to give his assent to A Petition of Rights Bill. This was designed to prevent further taxes without the authorisation of Parliament and imprisonment without due process.

In 1628, Sir John Heveningham stood again for Parliament. His stand against the forced loan had made him very popular and he was duly elected as Knight of the shire for Norfolk. In January 1629 a second sitting of Parliament took place where Sir John was able to take his seat.[11] During this session The Petition of Rights Bill was put to the King. The King's unhappiness with this Bill resulted in him dissolving Parliament and choosing to rule for the next eleven years without it. This is known as the personal rule of Charles I or the 'Eleven Years' of Tyranny'.

So ended Sir John's brief time as a Member of Parliament. The King had to reduce his expenditure and make peace with Spain and France.

Despite making peace with Spain and France the King was still short of money and looked for other income that would not involve a recall of Parliament. One such source was the Ship Money. This was a medieval system by which coastal towns and counties were required to provide for, or pay money towards, war ships. Charles introduced this as a form of general taxation. This caused resentment in the country. At Norwich in 1634 meetings were held to discuss how to raise the money for a warship. (William Heveningham, Sir Arthur's son, had been made High Sheriff of Norfolk in 1633.) The following year a second ship was funded and in 1636 yet another and another the following year, each ship costing approximately £5500. It was decided that this money would be found by contributions from Thetford, Castle-Rising and about 53 coastal towns in Norfolk raising £1271, Norwich £1601, King's Lynn £1192, Yarmouth £940 and Wisbech £340. This did not satisfy the Privy Council who demanded £1235 more. Norwich raised the money by a tax of 12d in the £ for lands, houses, gardens and stocks. The introduction of Ship Money was to result in Norwich favouring Parliament and resenting the King. Wymondham in 1635 paid £81 15s which was the fourth largest amount in Norfolk after Norwich, Lynn and Yarmouth. This was two-and-a-half times more than Thetford, suggesting Wymondham had become a prosperous town. Although Sir William Heveningham refused to pay the forced loan in 1637, he did allow royal agents onto his land to obtain saltpetre.[12]

The King appointed William Laud Archbishop of Canterbury in 1633. Laud wanted the church to follow a common practice of High Anglicanism with a greater importance placed on ceremony and the sacrament. This was not popular, creating concerns of a return to Catholic ways. At the Elizabethan settlement, the stone altar had been removed and a wooden communion table introduced. These were positioned in the nave, but Laud ordered them to be placed under the East window. The Bishop of Norwich, Matthew Wren, had to face the protest in Norfolk. He issued twenty-eight articles in an attempt to create uniformity in his diocese, including the requirement to place the communion table under the East window of the chancel.

William Heveningham had inherited Ketteringham Hall from his father in 1633 and with it he became patron of St Peter's although he did not have to present a vicar there until 1650 when he chose Miles Smith.[13] William Heveningham was a Presbyterian and an elder of a Presbyterian group of churches in Dunwich, Suffolk. As such he did not accept that the church was governed by a hierarchy of single bishops. It is likely that he took little interest in the running of the church and left the vicar, Richard Johnson, to undertake the requirement to move the communion table to a position under the East window where it has remained to this day.

In 1637, in an attempt to create a uniform church across Britain, Laud introduced his changes in Scotland. This included a new High Anglican Book of Common Prayer. Riots broke out in Edinburgh. In 1640 Charles led a force to subdue what has become known as the Bishops' War. This resulted in a truce between the two sides but another conflict followed, leading to a defeat for Charles who was then obliged to pay the Scots' war expenses. Charles was forced to turn to Parliament to raise money to suppress the Scottish rebellion.

Sir William Heveningham, who had followed his father and become an MP, attended this Parliament on behalf of Stockbridge, Hampshire. This was unusual as he rarely attended Parliament. Doubtless he shared the views of the MP John Pym, who led the criticism of the King for his actions during the time of his personal rule and his demand for ship money. Pym refused to discuss action in Scotland until these were settled. The King, not getting his way, dissolved Parliament in May after only a few weeks so giving it the name the Short Parliament. Despite not having the support of Parliament, Charles invaded Scotland only to be defeated resulting in the Scots occupying part of northern England. Yet another attempt of invasion by Charles, this time under the Earl of Stafford, again ended in failure and further parts of northern England fell under Scots' control. The costs of these wars, made worst because, as King of Scotland Charles was also paying the Scottish army, meant he had little choice but to summon Parliament again in the November of 1640.

This Parliament would become known as the Long Parliament as the Parliament agreed that it would not be dissolved unless its members agreed to do so. The Parliament attacked the King over his years of Personal Rule and then introduced measures to prevent it happening again. Thomas Wentworth, the Earl of Stafford and Archbishop Laud were impeached, Ship Money was abolished and it was agreed that taxes could only be levied with Parliamentary approval. Over the winter of 1641-2 the relationship between King and Parliament broke down. In January Charles arrived at Parliament with an armed guard to arrest John Pym and four other MPs. The MPs were not present having taken refuge so the King left. In March 1642, John Pym and his allies pushed through the Militia Ordinance (an Ordinance and not an Act of Parliament because it never received the Royal Assent). This Ordinance placed the command of each county's armed forces in the hands of their supporters. At the same time Charles I issued his own commissions of array assigning his followers to organise their own armed forces in the counties. The country was on the brink of civil war. The Civil War started on 22 August 1642 when Charles I raised his standard at Nottingham. He soon moved on to establish his headquarters at Oxford from where he controlled the west.

In October the first major battle took place at Edgehill ending in a draw. East Anglia largely supported Parliament and in December 1642 formed the Eastern Association. This was composed of the militias of the counties of Essex, Norfolk, Suffolk, Hertfordshire and Cambridgeshire, later joined by Huntingdonshire and Lincolnshire. Their role was to supply manpower and resources. Sir William Heveningham gave money for the garrison at Newport Pagnell which became a Parliamentary stronghold in 1644. Despite initial success for the Royalists in 1645; at the Battle of Naseby and the Battle of Langport the Parliamentarians destroyed Charles' armies. In summer 1646, the Royalists' headquarters in Oxford surrendered with Charles choosing to surrender to the Scots who handed him over to Parliament who imprisoned him.

At the start of the Civil War the Puritan MPs of the Long Parliament roughly divided into two groups, the Independents and the Presbyterians. The Independents (Congregationalists, Separatists) were a group who wanted the congregations of each church to be free to choose their own systems joining with others only by mutual agreement. The Presbyterians wanted a system similar to the Kirk in Scotland. The Presbyterians were willing to negotiate with the King to bring a quick peace while the Independents were prepared to fight to get what they wanted from a defeated King. Sir William Heveningham, despite being a Presbyterian, was generally considered to be an Independent in Parliament.

Charles escaped and made an agreement with the Scots that in return for the adoption of Presbyterianism, they should invade England. In 1648 a number of uprisings occurred throughout Britain in support of the King, the start of the Second Civil War. Norwich supported the Parliamentary and Royalists, such as the Mayor, were removed from positions of authority. Parliamentary troops were sent to the city to quell any riots. Elsewhere in Britain fighting was more serious; Parliamentary troops in Wales angry at not being paid joined the Royalists. Many battles took place and like the First Civil War the second went to the Parliamentarians.

Following the end of the Second Civil War, the Presbyterian majority of The Long Parliament attempted to negotiate with the King in the Treaty of Newport. This took place against a background of concerns regarding increasing radicalism of the New Model Army and their supporters in Parliament, the Independents. Discussions with the King broke down, but Parliament was reluctant to allow the army to seize the King. The next day Col. Thomas Pride and Lord Grey of Groby stood at the doors of the House of Commons refusing to allow the Presbyterian MPs to enter, later known as Pride's Purge. Sir William Heveningham, as an Independent, was allowed to enter. Without the Presbyterians the Independents were free to discuss the King's trial. Sir William Heveningham sided with the Independents supporting the army.

The following month, January 1649, Sir William Heveningham was voted a commissioner of the High Court for the trial of the King. He attended every session of the trial. His brother-in-law Robert Walpole was also a judge. Only a month after Pride's Purge, in January 1649 Charles I was tried and found guilty of treason. The judge announced to the court that Charles "shall be put to death

The Trial of Charles I at Westminster Hall, 1649.

by the severing of his head from his body". His death warrant was made ready on Monday, 29 January and signed by fifty-seven commissioners with a further ten being present but not signing. Sir William Heveningham was one who did not sign. When Parliament returned in the February 1649, he was one of the first MPs to certify his approval of the death sentence, as was required by Parliament.

Following the abolition of the monarchy and the House of Lords a Council of State was formed to act as the executive under Parliament. It consisted of forty-one councillors. Sir William Heveningham was appointed to the council in 1649 and 1650. After 1650 he appears to have become less involved in the running of the Commonwealth. He did, however, use this period as a time for money-making ventures. He bought properties confiscated from the church and Royalists' property such as Stanton Manor in 1653 and speculated in buying army indentures. His total annual income is estimated to have been £1000 per annum.[14]

From the execution of the King in 1649 to 1653, Britain experienced a period known as the Commonwealth. During the first few years of the Commonwealth unrest continued. A period referred to as the Third Civil War when the King's son, Charles, attempted to regain the throne with help from the Scots. This failed and Charles fled to France in 1651. In 1653 Cromwell disbanded the Rump Parliament and England became a Protectorate under Cromwell.

Civil War invariably causes the greatest loss of life of all conflicts. The English Civil War was the bloodiest in English history, killing a higher percentage of people than the First World War. Norfolk was not one of the major theatres of war, consequently few were killed and it is not known of any from Ketteringham. The only record of any military events close to Ketteringham was from a news sheet printed 29 August 1643 which records that 200 citizens from Norwich went almost as far as Wymondham to meet the Earl of Manchester and Col. Cromwell: "Soldiers out of Essex came to Norwich after the Earl, who as they came through Windham pulled down the organ in the church".[15]

After the Civil War the people of Ketteringham continued with that which mattered most to them, producing enough food and possibly a bit to spare. This they could sell or put to one side for the many festivals they enjoyed. During the Reformation their much-enjoyed feasts had been banned. Memories of this would return when, in 1641, sports were banned on the Sabbath, in 1645 holy days were banned and fast days introduced. The ban on feasts included Christmas celebrations.

The people of Ketteringham were not living in an isolated community. They shared a common with Wymondham and traded in its market and would likely be aware of an option that a few in the area chose, that of emigrating to America. Although there is no record of Ketteringham people emigrating it must have been a conversational piece when they returned from market. Some left from Wymondham. There is a Windham County in both Massachusetts and Connecticut. Between 1633 and 1640, 170 left from nearby Hingham for New England where, in 1635, Rev. Peter Hobart formed a Hingham in Massachusetts.[16] (A Hobart descendant would become the Vice-President of the United States.) In 1637 Samuel Lincoln arrived in 'New' Hingham. His great-great-great-great-grandson Abraham Lincoln would become the sixteenth president of the United States. Emigration was not necessarily as a direct result of the Civil War but a combination of persecution of the Puritans, poor harvest and general economic problems. The war, however, would no doubt have played its part in influencing some to leave.

It may appear that up to this point the Civil War had not been so bad for the Heveninghams. Sir William had risen to an important position in the new government and had made money out of the Parliamentary victory over the Royalists. This was true but not for all the family. Unlike Sir William his brother, Arthur Heveningham, had taken up the Royalist cause in the Civil War and was a Colonel at the Battle of Langport in 1645. This was a Parliamentary victory and Arthur was taken prisoner and fined £400. He was fined an additional £600 for receiving the privy seal of Charles I at Oxford. This left Arthur's side of the Heveningham family impoverished. While dying at his home in Hockwold in 1657 he left his wife, Jane and children in the care of his brother, Sir William at Ketteringham. Within two months Sir William had turned them out to find shelter elsewhere. It is said that, but for a friend taking them in they would have died. The family had been torn apart by the war. In 1674 Matthew Goodrick wrote to Sir William Heveningham mentioning that his brother asked to be forgiven.[17]

Cromwell died in 1658 and was succeeded by his son Richard who was deposed the following year. Parliament invited Charles to return from exile and he was crowned Charles II in 1660. At the Restoration Sir William's sister-in law, who along with her children he had turned away from Ketteringham Hall three years earlier, was granted £200 from the Ketteringham estate.[18]

With his return, the King's thoughts of revenge against those who had his father killed could be put into action. The regicides were tracked down, Sir William Heveningham was imprisoned in Windsor Castle. While there he petitioned the House of Lords four times for mercy. He claimed he had been generous to his loyalist brother Arthur and his widow Jane. Sir William died still imprisoned in Windsor in 1677.[19]

The Heveningham widows had been left to manage their estates. Arthur Heveningham's estate in Hockwold became the responsibility of his widow Jane's second son, Henry, who was only 9 years old at the Restoration. He inherited the Suffolk estate in 1678 but chose to live at Hockwold.[20] Lady Mary Heveningham had the problem of being the wife of a regicide. At his imprisonment Sir William was deprived of his estates, however, on 26 September 1661 the Crown made a grant to Brian, Viscount Cullen, and four others as trustees for Lady Mary to recover the estate.

Lady Mary, having saved the family estate at Ketteringham, and knowing it was safe for her heirs, chose to reside at her house in Jermyn Street, London where she died 19 January 1696. Her will reminds us that it was a time when the loss of a child was common. Lady Mary had lost her first-born son, Carey. She intended to leave the Ketteringham and Heveningham estates to her second son, William. He had married Barbara, the daughter of George Villiers, the 3rd Viscount's grandson. William died soon after his father Sir William in 1678 leaving his daughter, Abigail, as next in-line to inherit the Ketteringham Estate. As well as two sons Sir William and Lady Mary had a daughter, Abigail who married Sir John Newton, but she had died ten years before her brother William. Abigail, her niece, had married Henry Heron following the death of her grandmother Lady Mary.

Henry Heron became the new Lord of the manor living there for 20 years. He was elected MP for Boston in 1713 and was described in a Tory newspaper as: "of very ancient and loyal family, son to Sir Henry Heron... who attended and served King Charles I in all his troubles, is worthy of such a father, continuing steadfast to all loyal and generous principles".[21]

It would appear that Abigail Heron was not tainted by her grandfather's role in King Charles' execution. Henry and Abigail had a son Heveningham Heron in the March 1701. He was baptised at St Peter's, Ketteringham but no other mention is made of him and it is assumed he died young. The following year Henry and Abigail had a daughter, Barbara, who, in 1714 married (it is said against the wishes of her parents) a guardsman named Frampton. During his time at Ketteringham Hall, Henry Heron presented the following vicars to the living; in 1697, Richard Clark, in 1707, Nathaniel Saltier who resigned in 1716 and was replaced by Thomas Tunstall.

In 1717 Henry Heron sold the Ketteringham estate to Sir Edward Atkyns bringing to an end 225 years of Heveninghams at Ketteringham. Abigail Heron died in 1735, her daughter Barbara had died in 1721 and with them all memories of Ketteringham.

Notes

1. Hunter, *The History and Topography of Ketteringham in the county of Norfolk*, p.43.
2. Blomefield, *An Essay Towards A Topographical History of the County of Norfolk*: vol. 5, p.93.
3. Ibid. 1, p.44.
4. Ibid. 2, p.93.
5. Smith, *County and Court Government and Politics in Norfolk 1558- 1603*, p.157.
6. Ibid., p.159.
7. Ibid., p.329.
8. Ibid. 2, p.93.
9. Ibid. 2, p.94.
10. History of Parliament,entry for Heveningham, Sir John Heveningham.
11. Ibid.
12. Ibid.
13. Ibid. 2, p.52.
14. *Oxford Dictionary of National Biography* 13142.
15. Barringer & Fowle, *Wymondham in the 17cent.*, p.63.
16. History Group of the Hingham Society, *Hingham The American Connection from the earliest settlers to the present day*, p.10-12.
17. Ibid. 10, entry for Heveningham, Henry.
18. Ibid.
19. *Dictionary of National Biography, 1885-1900*, entry for Heveningham, William.
20. Hockwold parish register records several people with the surname Ketteringham. It is possible that some villagers from Ketteringham choose to relocate due to their Royalist sympathies.
21. Ibid. 10, entry for Heron, Henry.

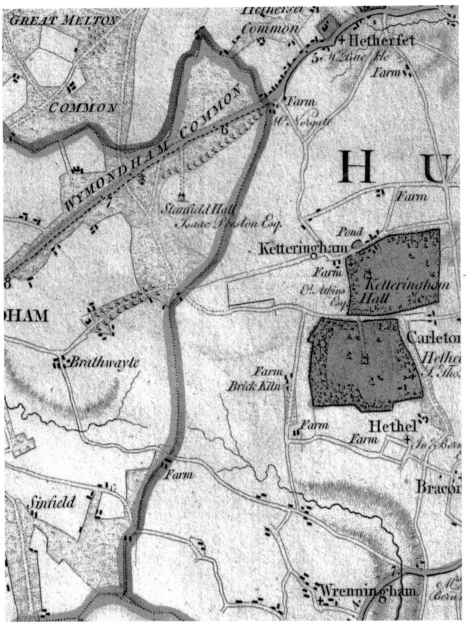

Faden's 1797 map of Norfolk, showing Ketteringham.

Ketteringham at the time of the Heveninghams

The Heveninghams made Ketteringham Hall their family seat and quite successfully pursued their political ambitions by gaining greater influence and status. To achieve this, Ketteringham Hall needed to be transformed from a medieval manor house to a residence that not only reflected their rising fortunes but displayed the higher status they desired. This required the Hall to be greatly improved. A grand building needs to be set in equally impressive grounds. The need to impress would also require changes being made to Ketteringham village.

The changes they made were primarily for their own benefit, however, many of these did affect the ordinary folk of Ketteringham. Their story, often lacking perceived significance and available evidence, is often ignored. But it can be argued that their story is as important a part of the village's history as that of those who dwelt at the Hall. For the majority of those who lived in Ketteringham, both at this time and for later generations, what was most important was producing sufficient food for their families. How the village changed with regards to growing food gives an insight into the impact on the wider village population. In medieval times food was grown within a system of open field farming. For this system to function, access to and use of a common was needed. The common rights had been agreed in medieval times, long before the Heveninghams inherited the manor. These rights remained and would remain as long as the common existed. The medieval open field farming had been replaced but what of the medieval common? How much existed when the Heveninghams inherited the manor, and how much was lost during their ownership of the manor?

There are a few later maps which, when combined with some landscape analysis, provide an indication as to how and why the common changed. We are also fortunate in having a piece of documentary evidence from the mid-16th century giving details of the common.

In 1536 Sir John Heveningham died and was buried in Ketteringham church. Following his death an inquisition was held in the Shire House, Norwich. The inquest details his possessions as follows: The manor of Ketteringham and that, which goes with it, eight messuages [1] 300 acres of land,100 acres of meadow, 300 acres of pasture, 60 acres of wood, 40 acres of heath, 20 acres of marsh, £10 rent from Ketteringham, Carlton and Hethersett.[2]

The common was an area of heavy land unsuitable for arable cultivation and a part of the boulder clay plateau which runs north-west to south-east through

Norfolk. The clay subsoil is impermeable making for wet land, evidence of which can be seen by 20 acres being recorded as marsh at the inquisition. 40 acres are described as heath which would have been common land used for grazing and 60 acres were wood. Combining heath, marsh and wood there were only 120 acres of common remaining by the mid-16th century. The earliest document we have on Ketteringham is the Domesday Book of 1086. Although it does not directly mention the common, my analysis of the information it does provide suggests a common of around 350 to 400 acres.[3] Two-thirds of the common had disappeared in the 450 years since Domesday. Before considering how that might have happened, I want to consider the 120 acres that remained in 1536.

The common may have long gone but the land remains farmland to this day. Smeeth Wood, known locally as the Smee is around 60 acres. In 1837 the Ketteringham Estate was sold at auction. The sale details provided both map and details of the various parcels of land included in the sale[4]. Smeeth Wood is catalogued as sixty-six acres two roods and one perch. [5] The wood appears on the earliest maps of the area[6] confirming it is the same wood mentioned in 1536. This makes Smeeth Wood around five hundred years old. The official definition of ancient woodland is woodland dating back to AD 1600 a definition Smeeth Wood meets, making it one of the few pockets of ancient woodland remaining in Norfolk. It is possibly the only piece of land in the village that has never been put to the plough and cultivated. Its name, Smeeth, would suggest grazing land but

Standing water on former common. An indicating of heavy soil.

more likely the name derives from, the land, or wood, on the grazing land. A 19th century field adjacent to the wood was known as the Smeeth, a possible legacy of a larger grazing area near the wood. Other field names in use in the 19th century still carried reference to the common. A narrow field, resembling a track, which lead from Low Street to the field called Smeeth was called, Common Piece, a name derived from a time when the villagers had a shared access path (common access) to the common for grazing.

Sir John Heveningham's inquest records forty acres of heath in Ketteringham. The earliest map on which Ketteringham is shown was on one of a range of maps of Norfolk published in 1797 by William Faden.[7] One map shows Wymondham Common and what remained of Ketteringham Common. It is not a detailed map and surprisingly does not show High Ash Farm, and places Stanfield Hall on Wymondham Common *(see p.34)*. However, if details on Faden's map are transcribed onto the sales map of 1837 *(see below)* it is possible to suggest the extent of the common in 1797. When measured, this area is very close to 40 acres which suggests this was the common in 1536 and remained as common land until the end of the 18th century. Bryant produced a similar map to Faden's in 1826.[8] This showed that none of the once great common on the heavy land between Wymondham and Ketteringham remained. In less than thirty years the medieval common would be no more, but that would happen after the Heveninghams.

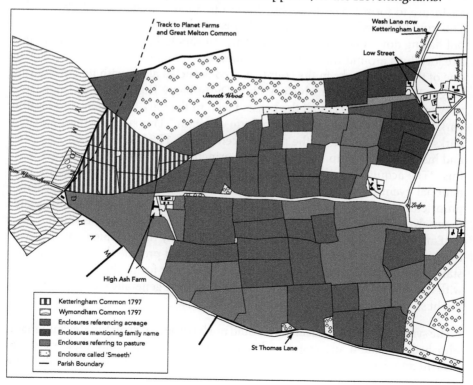

1837 Estate map

The reduction in size of this important feature resulted from changes in agriculture practice and the economic structure of Ketteringham. Many of these have their origins before the Heveninghams arrived, but to appreciate their Ketteringham and understand the evolution of Ketteringham as an estate village it is beneficial to consider the reduction of the common without the restriction of a time frame.

Young deer near the former common, 2022.

The fortunate few with large landholdings saw these as means of producing wealth and status. Those whose landholding included common land were limited as to the wealth it could generate but could use it to raise their status. At various locations on the perimeter of the greater common, of which Ketteringham's was only a small part, high ranking families carved out areas to create deer parks. These were highly desirable as they provided both status and food. On the large expanse of common herds of red and roe deer had roamed since the end of the last Ice Age. By building a fence, known as a pale, around an area of woodland it was possible to drive wild deer into a large enclosure to form a deer park. In addition to a fence a ditch might also be dug. This could be used to create a 'leap', that is an obstacle that deer could leap over but having done so could not return. This appears to have taken place at four or five locations around this expanse of common. At Silfield Common (Oxehaghe), one of the largest parks in the county was constructed along with its own hunting lodge. A charter exists in which William De Aubigny II grants to the monastery at Wymondham, tithes of all the beasts taken in the park Oxehaghe and another park centred on Grishaugh, Wymondham common.[9] This suggests these two deer parks were in existence by the mid-12th century. In 1265 Sir Reginald Argentine and his wife Lora set up residence at Ketteringham Hall. Joseph Hunter writes of this, "The acquisition of Ketteringham Hall by the family of Argentine is a most material event in its history".[10] His reasoning was they were not just "absentee proprietors… (who) merely derived an income from Ketteringham but seated themselves there".[11] It was now the home of a knight who was the son-in-law of an Earl which no doubt might have resulted in many improvements being made to the hall. A deer park adjacent to the house would provide the new home with status. Ketteringham's deer park boundary follows or forms the parish boundary with that of East Carleton. As parish boundaries were generally fixed by 1180, this might suggest the park existed before that date.[12]

The symbolic status of a deer park would not have been lost on the Heveninghams who had become a successful and important family. Naturally they wished to present an image that reflected this. The old deer park was tucked out of the way, far from Ketteringham Hall at the edge of the common. This was fine when it was a resource for food and timber, but this location may not have projected the trappings of success and importance they might have desired. The deer park was probably enlarged as part of a new layout of the grounds of Ketteringham Hall taking place to reflect the grandeur of a new Elizabethan Hall. This the Heveninghams had built in the late 16th century. The boundary, pale, of the early deer parks can still be seen as a ditch

Inner-park wood boundary ditch, 2022.

marking Inner-park Wood. To the west of this is another ditch that marks Outer Park Wood and is the probable pale of the new deer park

Although the deer park was a more substantial enclosure of the common it was not responsible for the major reduction in size. There are two more important reasons, both of which can be deduced from the 1837 Estate sale map *(see p.37).*[13] Although drawn long after the common had disappeared much remained of the medieval farming landscape. It is possible to identify the original medieval strips and how they had been combined to create enclosures. In the sale document the farm descriptions use the term enclosure, however, when itemised they are invariable called closes. To avoid confusion when discussing enclosure of the common I will use the term close when referring to an open field enclosure. The closes near the settlement, at the end of High Street, display the irregular boundaries, some with curves, as seen elsewhere in the village. The curved edges I attribute to the open field farming and the need, in medieval times, to turn a team of oxen in preparation to cut the next furrow.[14] These closes, however, differ from the majority of closes in that on the western side they are orientated at right angles to the road. Generally, when a road exists or is constructed the boundaries are perpendicular to the road whereas roads built through an existing field structure are not. The relationship between road closes on the western side suggests they are contemporary with the road. The route of the original medieval road was to the church so it can be assumed that this is a later road *(see p.18)*. The original road was part of a network that skirted the common. The new road is evidence of the common edge moving further west. The southern end of the road once ran further to the east and was likely moved when Wymondham lodge was built. These closes are part of one phase of enclosure where dwellings, having moved to the common edge, began enclosing areas of the adjacent common.

The 1837 map identifies each of these enclosures by name. These have names such as: Grove Close, Oakey Close and Spinks Eden. Those with a family name are located close to dwellings at the end of High Street *(see map on p.37)*.

The junction of High Street and the common perimeter track (now Low Street and Ketteringham Lane) was a crossway with High Street continuing onto the common. The access track was still referred to in the 19th century as 'common piece', because it was the piece of land that provided access to the common or, it was a piece of land, common to all, for access. This led to a long thin strip of land known as the Smeeth. Smeeth implies grazing. The next three sections form a band that curves round the edge of Smeeth Wood before joining the common of 1797. This appears to be the route taken by medieval villagers to the common. In 1836 a notice appeared in the Norfolk Chronicle announcing the intention to move a footpath in Ketteringham. In describing the location of the footpath it refers to an ancient drift way that ran from the end of High Street into Smeeth Wood.[15] A drift way is a way for flocks and herds to access the common.

The common was, by 1536, a mere 40 acres. The enclosure on the eastern edge accounted for only a small proportion of the former common. The loss of the remaining occurred for another reason. An indication of how and why might be seen in the remaining enclosure names. Although it must be remembered these names are taken from a document complied 300 years after Heveningham's inquest, names are often a good indication of contemporary and earlier use. The names which describe an enclosure as pasture are coloured pink and those only described by acreage are coloured orange. The enclosures described as grazing form an area on the east edge of the old common similar to those closes given personal names but to the south. The choice of land use is largely dictated by the type of soil and how wet the area is. Pasture is grazing land and should not be too wet. The location near to the village was probably drained and enclosed early on. The most westerly field in this patch of grazing was called Fir Pasture. Fir referring not to pine trees but furze or gorse pasture, a species common on the heath. The enclosures beyond those known as pasture are named purely by their acreage with names such as The Five Acres, The Middle Six Acres and Further Six Acres. These functional names are often found where a large area of uncultivated land becomes available and can be divided into suitable areas. Once it is decided to create a five acre field its name, with no other history, is given. Uncultivated land might have indicated the enclosure of common land, however as most had disappeared by 1536, it was probably a large expanse of pastureland.

Enclosing common land for grazing livestock by landowners had been frequent practice since the medieval period. As the owner of the common, Lords of the Manor would consider the best way of deriving the greatest income from the manor. Following the Norman conquest, the new Norman Lords Bigod and Peverel, on replacing the Saxon thanes Ulf and Ketil, gave consideration as to how their newly acquired manors might produce the greatest financial returns. One that is clear from the Domesday record was the introduction of sheep. None are recorded in Anglo Saxon Kitrincham but 120 appear after the Norman Conquest.

The common remained because it was unsuitable for arable farming. It was an asset to the villagers but most of the benefit they derived from it was difficult to tax so provided limited financial reward for the Lord. The value of rearing sheep was not as now for the meat, but for the fleece. With a monetary value this could be taxed, or if the flock of sheep belonged to the Lord all profit would be his. The common offered a large expanse of land that could be used for grazing. Sheep feet suffer on wet land so the predominately wet areas of common would be unsuitable for sheep grazing, but the financial benefits of keeping sheep would be justification for draining parts of the common. This was likely a piecemeal process which had, by the arrival of the Heveninghams, resulted in a much reduced common. The majority of common was no longer of benefit to the villagers but was now generating an income for the Heveninghams.

To convert wet heavy common land to pasture drainage work is required. Drainage work had been carried out since medieval times, but this was likely a small local piecemeal process. The financial benefit of sheep resulted in a coordinated approach to the issue of drainage. At the turn of the 17th century, however, 20 acres were still wet enough to be recorded as marsh. Today, roughly in the centre of the former common, is a pond from which drainage ditches flow in and out as they drain into the river Tiffey to the south. This is the highest point in Ketteringham and is, therefore, not the expected location for a pond. This is a feature found in the local landscape where, at the high points, the clay layer is closest to the surface resulting in the water table coming close to the surface (a perched water-table) creating an area of wetland. Although only a pond today, it is possibly all that remains of a former large expanse of marsh land. Despite being a large area, at 20 acres, it may have been the remains of a larger marsh which was at that time reducing following drainage work. The field where the pond occurs was known as the 'Further Five Acres' possibly being named as the area was drained it gave a further five acres. This work had been complete by 1797 when Faden's map showed no remaining marshland.

As commons were enclosed it became possible to create new roads. As the common was owned by a single individual and there were no dwellings, tofts and field boundaries to take into account they could take the most direct and convenient routes. This was invariably a straight line. A new straight road was created from Ketteringham to the important town market of Wymondham. Before this was constructed, St Thomas Lane was the only road. This follows Ketteringham's southern boundary and

High Ash Road crosses the former common, 2022.

was possibly the common boundary track. The point, where it becomes straight (*see map below, enclosure 78*) is where, in medieval times, it would have continued to Ketteringham church.

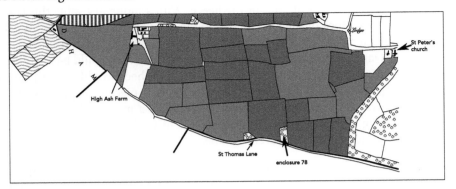

The boundaries on either side of the enclosure road are perpendicular to the road indicating the two are contemporary. This would be the case if the common was being enclosed. If, as I believe, it had already been turned to pasture, the road is more likely to pre-date the boundaries. The road may relate to the change from common to pasture and the subsequently required drainage work. The road provides access to High Ash farm. The current farmhouse dates to the 16th century[16] which may be an indication as to the enclosure road's age. The width from hedge to hedge is typically 100ft resulting in the verges on either side of the road (now called High Ash Road) being the largest of any in the village. Up until 1790 enclosures roads were required to be at least 60 ft wide. This was to spread the ware caused by livestock over a wider area. Despite the drainage work this road was likely still very wet in winter and as it was the main route to Wymondham market. Its great width would go some way to limiting the damage that many hooves might cause. The combined area of the of the verges would be recorded in the sales map two hundred years later as nearly five acres. There were once gates at either end of the road to contain livestock. The verges supplying summer grazing and a convenient means of keeping the road's vegetation under-control.

High Ash Road has a 'kink' as it crosses the Ketteringham / Wymondham parish boundary. The reason for this is apparent when Faden's map is consulted. Although High Ash Road could be straight up to the parish boundary over the boundary was Wymondham Common, here it required a gentle curve to meet up with a later enclosure road. The piecemeal

Map showing parish boundary between Ketteringham and Wymondham.

enclosure process between the parishes is evident. This differs from the old A11 (B1172) which keeps its straight course at it crosses the Wymondham-Hethersett parish boundary. This enclosure road was the result of parliamentary enclosures of the common in the late 18th, early 19th century.[17]

Faden's map shows that the large areas of common were crossed by tracks which not only provided access to the common but connected communities on different parts of the common edge. St Thomas Lane is shown as a track which continued northward across both the remaining Ketteringham Common and Wymondham Common to join the Wymondham to Hethersett road. The track then continued across Great Melton Common to Great Melton. The track provides access to Planet Farm (formally Plainwood Farm) which is located just north of Smeeth Wood on the edge of Norwich Common. Planet Farm has a 17th century thatched barn[18] so the farm would have existed in the time of the Heveningham and is one of many dwellings shown on Faden's map around the edge of Wymondham Common.

On Norwich Common, near where the St Thomas Lane track would have met the Wymondham to Hethersett road was a windmill. It is possible that farmers in Ketteringham took their grain for grinding here. One of fields near Five Ways was once called Windmill Hill. Despite being an ideal location, I have found no evidence of a windmill here or anywhere else in Ketteringham.

During this period it became possible to prosper and become rich through trade and commerce without the need for large land holdings. To be a member of the gentry, however, it was a requirement to have large land holdings. Sir John Heveningham had owned 700 acres in Ketteringham plus 120 acres of common. When William Peach sold the estate in 1837, the parish measured 1606 acres and he would have owned all of it. The freemen who had cultivated the individual strips in medieval times owned their strips, but those who worked the 'enclosures' on the 1837 sale document did not. The amount owned by Sir John is recorded as 700 acres plus the common. He is also recorded as having the manor of Ketteringham with the appurtenances which were likely to include the gardens and parkland of the Hall and the enlarged deer park. This may have added an additional two hundred acres to his holding. The Hall also owned eight messuages which would have had their own land. How much is not known. The building that would become High Ash farmhouse has a worn stone bearing the initials of Sir John Heveningham's great, great grandson William Heveningham the earlier building was probably one of these messuages. Its holding would possibly include much of the former common. Sir John Heveningham would have owned about two thirds of the parish at his death in 1536 and it is assumed his family descendants acquired more during their time at Ketteringham Hall.

A man or woman born when the Heveninghams moved into Ketteringham Hall would by the time they were fifty have seen the price of grain triple. By 1650 it would double again to be eight times the price in 1500.[19] As land brought in greater wealth, the larger farms became more profitable and were able to use their wealth to buy more land. Livestock prices showed a similar growth, although wool price rises were modest by comparison. Small landowners in hard times might sell to a wealthy neighbour and move to the town or city. The population of Norwich rose from around 10,000 in 1500 to 16,000 in 1580.[20] The population of England rose from 3 million in 1550 to over 5 million in 1650.[21] This may be why some of the field names carry the names of families who disappeared from the parish records. History tends to record the successful by name and forget or ignore those left at the bottom and there must have been a large number who did not prosper. They laboured in the enclosures of Ketteringham, but we know little of them.

Before considering how the Heveninghams used their increased wealth to improve their home, I wish to return briefly to the ordinary folk of Ketteringham. At the start of the chapter, I mentioned that for the villagers of Ketteringham the two most important aspect of the village were growing sufficient food and the church. That is because both offered the possibility of survival from their two greatest fears, hunger and illness. As farmers the land provided the food to prevent hunger and a possible surplus to sell for additional food. The church was important as a means of reducing the fear of illness. It attempted to understand why people became ill, provided the rituals to prevent illness and comfort, hope and reassurance for a better life in the next world. The illness they feared the most was the plague. The parish records show that in 1604 from July to October twelve people died, largely from the families Peel and Page.[22] This concentration of death in two months suggests plague. Ketteringham was not far from Norwich which, after London, was the largest city in the country. As a port and centre of commerce and administration it was always susceptible to infections. It suffered plague in 1625/6 killing 1431people. In 1630 and again 1636 the plague returned. It can be assumed the infection travelled into nearby villages including Ketteringham.

A chapter entitled Ketteringham at the time of the Heveninghams' would not be complete without considering the buildings that existed at this time. These buildings provide a visual and tangible connection with that time. They also have their own story that adds to the greater history of Ketteringham. At the centre of the village was Ketteringham Hall. The building we see today was rebuilt and remodelled by the architects Allason and Jekyll in the Gothic style following a fire in the 19th century. The stables, banqueting hall and conservatory were added at this time. It is believed that the core of the building is of Tudor origin. Few details and no images exist of this building but it appears to have been a half 'H' shape which was later filled in during Jekyll's modifications in 1852. Blomefield states that William Heveningham repaired the house in 1648. A letter from Mathew Goodrick mentions 200,000 bricks "burnt" at Ketteringham in the summer of 1674 and the construction of a new staircase that, 'I hope to see it as hansome a stayrecase for its size, as any in England'.[23] It would appear the Heveninghams were intent on making their family seat worthy of their aspirations in society.

Such grandeur for the house also requires an equally grand setting. Blomefield notes that when William Heveningham improved the house, he also made a plantation of trees. Which plantation this refers to is not clear but was likely part of greater improvements to the setting of Ketteringham Hall.

The lower lake, 2006.

The two lakes we see today were part of a late 18th century garden design. This might well have been an update of the layout introduced by the Heveninghams. The lower lake probably dates to Anglo-Saxon times. Domesday records a mill in Ketteringham in the late Anglo-Saxon period. As the only accessible flowing water it would suggest this was the location of the water mill. The brook was dammed to create a mill pond. The mill was abandoned at the Norman conquest. The mill pond later becoming the lower lake. There is a map of Ketteringham Hall grounds when in the ownership of Mrs Atkyns, from 1750, which shows a formal park with the belts of trees in place. The lakes are rectangular in shape formal, as opposed to the naturalistic layout that would be preferred by later owners. It is quite possible the layout was that introduced by the Heveninghams. The neighbouring Hethel Hall belonged to Sir Thomas Beevor. Hethel Park depicted on Faden's map was slightly larger than Ketteringham's *(see p.34)* and a mid-18th century map shows it landscaped. With the Heveningham's desire to impress it is probable that they would want theirs to be as fine as their neighbours.

The terrace at the south of the Hall was added to provide a place to view the park with steps leading down to the water. On the terrace there was perhaps a knot garden, so favoured by the Tudors with some topiary and lawns where games like bowls could be played, and beyond the deer park. The enlarged deer park gave visual enhancement and status when the Heveningham's entertained.

The western extant of the deer park onto the common has been discussed but the eastern boundary or pale is not clear. It likely that it no longer functioned as a deer park. The only deer being wild herds. Faden's map of 1797 shows the park land, extending to 19th century boundaries defined by belts of trees. The south-east boundary, known as Ladybelt, is overlaid on earlier field boundaries. One was called Ludgate suggesting there was a back

The south terrace, 2006.

gate here. About midway in Ladybelt are several small leaved lime trees which were once coppiced. The size of the stools would suggest they are at least four hundred years old and therefore could have been planted when the grounds were laid out by the Heveninghams. Lime is not a hedgerow tree. Lime is sensitive to grazing which would have made it an odd choice if it was still a deer park. Lime is a woodland tree which might suggest it is a remnant of former woodland, but the field boundaries do not suggest any woodland and Faden's map does not show any woodland in Ketteringham Park. It is quite possible that the park was extended to the tree belt by the Heveninghams. Several well-established parkland limes exist beyond the lower lake.

The oldest building in Ketteringham is St Peter's church. The relationship between the church and the Hall has ranged from moral superiority to subservience. Those who dwelt at the Hall considered it to be their private chapel and those who inhabited the rectory or vicarage quietly accepted that due to the patronage that flowed from the Hall. The church Thomas Heveningham inherited had benefited from Sir Henry Grey's patronage. Richard Bocher was the priest and would remain so until 1501.[24] The early years of Heveninghams at the Hall were, for St Peter's, uneventful. The following fifty years were far from that as the Crown and the Church sorted, or attempted to sort, their relationship. This would have profound implications for churches in all communities. How St Peter's weathered the storm will be discussed later.

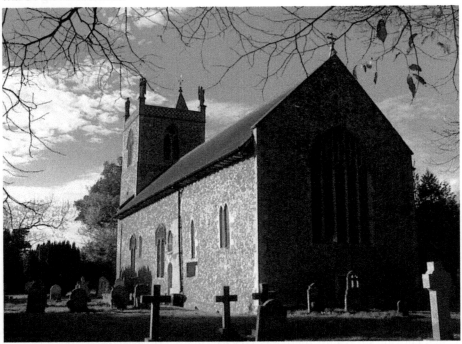

St Peter's Church, 2004.

One change in the relationship between Ketteringham Hall and St Peter's was who held the advowson. This was the right to appoint the priest, or vicar, to St Peter's. Like the Greys, the Heveninghams may have viewed St Peter's as their private chapel, but the vicar who presided over it was appointed by another. This no doubt caused the status seeking Heveninghams great frustration. Following the dissolution of the religious houses, including Pentney Priory which held the advowson, Robert Rumbald (Reyanbald, Reynbald) brought the rectory and lands in 1545.[25] and with them the right to appoint the vicar. Robert Rumbald was not from a family of gentry intent on increasing his land holding. He was a grocer in Norwich. The right to appoint the vicar residing with a grocer may have added to the Heveningham's frustration, but it did save them from the difficult job of finding a vicar. Ketteringham was a poor benefice and therefore not popular and difficult to fill. Following Richard Haggar's death in 1558 it took four years to find a replacement, that being John Dixy who remained until 1568 when Adam Each was appointed. The position lapsed and the advowson was sold to a gentleman by the name of Andrew Thetford. He appointed Henry Webb on 1576 who resigned in 1584. Andrew Thetford was then joined by Thomas Thetford and together they appointed Robert Grey and two years later William Parry. William was uncommitted to Ketteringham and, because of this, he neglected his position as resident priest. His role was then taken by The Queen. Andrew and Thomas then presented Robert Jackler who resigned in 1602 and was replaced by Richard Parker. Thomas Thetford appears to have found the task of finding suitable priests to take on the living at Ketteringham a difficult one. He chose to sell the advowson to Sir Henry Hobart of Blickling Hall and Intwood, Sir William Paston and a group of trustees for the use of Sir John Heveningham who, in 1611 presented Richard Johnson AM. Sir John's father Sir Arthur Heveningham was Lord of the Manor at this time and would remain so until 1630. It was not purchased for his use but for his son. Sir John married Sir William Paston's daughter, Bridget in 1601 so rather than a snub to Sir Arthur it was likely a gift to Sir William's son-in-law.

Richard Johnson AM is the first vicar at St Peter's to be recorded as having a degree. The letters AM (which we would now reverse) after his name indicate, Master of Arts. With Ketteringham's difficulties in attracting vicars to the parish it would appear unusual that he chose St Peter's. The reason may be both Richard and Sir Henry attended Queens' College, Cambridge at a similar time. He remained as vicar for 39 years—an exceptionally long period for Ketteringham. It is not clear if any inducements were given to entice him to come to this poor living and stay for so long. There was work carried out on the vicarage at this time. The

Church Cottage, 2022.

original building was a hall house which, in the 17th century, had a chimney and an upper floor added. Since 1559 the clergy had been allowed to marry. Richard Johnson was a family man having six children although two died at birth. The new upper floor would have added useful additional space. Whether this was for the benefit of Sir John's fellow Cambridge alumnus is unknown. The glebe terrier for 1635 records a further six acres of land for the vicar in addition to the twenty-six acres of glebe. It is possible that the Heveninghams made additional land available to the vicar to make life easier for him. This land is not included in glebe terriers after Richard Johnson's time.

In 1623 Sir Arthur Heveningham became impropriator and patron of St Peter's, although he never had the opportunity to appoint an incumbent as the Rev. Johnson held the post for 39 years. Sir Arthur's nephew, Sir William had the honour of being the first at Ketteringham Hall in five hundred years to appoint a vicar when, in 1650, he appointed Miles Smith.

St Peter's had a patron, the importance of which for a poor living like Ketteringham cannot be underestimated. It is not possible to give any exact value of the patronage, but it must have been a comfort to the vicar knowing the patron next door was both wealthy and influential. Post Reformation, and the lack of belief in purgatory, the desire to give money to the priest to say prayers for the dead had gone. However, Sir Arthur Heveningham's sister Francis left in her will "to Mr Johnson vicar of Ketteringham three pounds in money"[26] in 1643, the Lady Mary Heveningham left £10 to the then vicar.[27] These gifts suggest gratitude to the vicar who they viewed as their vicar looking after their church and almost a member of the family. Such generosity does not appear to have been part of Sir Arthur character if his dealings with the church tower are anything to go by. In 1608 a storm damaged the church tower. In the parish register, the vicar, Richard Parker records, "Ketteringham steeple fell in the night season, being a very calm night, the 20 of July 1608. The whole foot of the font was removed a foot breadth from his place: … yea, all the bells were whole and not one of them broken". Amusingly a contemporary added: "He might have put in that the steeple fell, and he laying in the vicarage (next door) heard it not"[28] a possible suggestion he was sleeping off the drink.

Arthur Heveningham provided the bricks and timber for the repair and fed the carpenters and masons, but he decided their wages would be paid by a compulsory levy on his servants, Ketteringham's parishioners and his friends and family. He added to this money from the county treasury which he had voted through. He recorded those who gave to the repair in a town book but, in addition, he added a list of names headed "all these did give noe monye and the most parte of them did nothinge ells about this good worke as all the rest of the townes men doe know".[29]

It is possible that St Peter's had a pulpit in earlier times but, following the reformation, with its emphasis on the priest communicating with the congregation, a pulpit was expected. The pulpit became more central to the church service, a place where not only a sermon could be preached but a reading from the bible could be made. The current three-decker pulpit in St Peter's supplies a place for both, and it is possible, that the pulpit that existed in the 17th century did likewise. To listen to the sermon, pews were installed where people sat according to their 'place' in society. The square box pew, used by the Boileau family in the 19th century, is still in place and it is likely a similar arrangement existed for the Heveninghams. A priest door existed where the vestry passage is now. Above the door is a plaque dated 1684. This is followed by the initials MH, possibly Mary Heveningham. The rood beam is of 17th century style and was likely replaced in the reign of Charles I or II.[30]

The rectory is 16th century but is on the site of a much earlier building. St Peter's had been appropriated to Pentney Priory since 1140. The Prior had the living as Rector and appointed a resident priest or vicar. The Prior took the great tithes leaving the lesser tithes to the vicar for his work. This resulted in Ketteringham becoming a poor living. The Prior provided a house for the vicar and a house for himself as rector. Although the buildings we see today are not the original buildings they do give an indication of differential in wealth. The vicarage is a timber framed building whereas the rectory is grander and built of brick. The vicarage was built next to the church underlining how the rector saw the vicar's position whereas the rector's house is set back at a respectable distance facing both church and vicarage.

The buildings covered so far belonged to people whose names and lives we have a record. The next group of houses we only know what the building might tell. Today we judge a property's value by the adage 'location, location, location'. The village migrated before the Heveninghams to a 'desirable' location on the common edge where there was convenient access to the common. This tells us how important the common once was, but in addition, may suggest something else. Where the access road to the common, Low Street, meets the common perimeter road, Ketteringham Lane, there are four houses that date back to the Heveningham period: Wellgate Cottage(s),[31] the Thatched Cottage, Avon Cottage and Bridge Cottage. Until the 1960's there was another 16th century cottage (Horseshoe Cottage) on Low Street where the modern chalet bungalow now stands. Taking this bungalow (with the wonderful name Cytringa) as the centre point for a circle with a radius of 350 feet the other four properties fall on the perimeter of the circle. This may be mere coincidence, or it might suggest planning and an agreement between landowners. If the five cottages were part of the eight messuages recorded as part of Sir John Heveningham's estate, then the Heveninghams or Greys, if they replaced an earlier building, may have over seen their location. It may be a step too far to describe Ketteringham as a planned estate village but if planning was involved, it is an indication of the control the Lord had on the manor.

The oldest house in Ketteringham, is Wellgate Cottage(s). When first built in the

Wellgate Cottages

late 15th century it was an open hall with a central hearth. The hearth was later replaced by a chimney and in the late 16th century a floor was added to create a second floor. It is likely that a parlour was also added around this time[32]. Avon Cottage is 16th century and, although now three cells may once have been a single hall[33]. The Thatched Cottage is also 16th century and Bridge Cottage is believed to date from 1624. Although this is the youngest of this group it, and the others for that matter, might have been on the site of earlier dwellings.[34]

Along High Street away from the common is Juniper Cottage. The house we see today dates from the 17th century.[35] Further along High Street is Ivy House Farmhouse. It was built around 1530.[36] It is a mile from the common edge, an indication that by the early 16th century the common's importance was diminishing. Its location away from the common does not appear to have been too detrimental as it was extended in the late 17th early 18th century. It is likely that this was one Sir John Heveningham's eight messuages.

High Ash Farmhouse dates from the 16th century.[37] Built on the former common it is a grand building and was intended to make a statement. Travelling from Wymondham it was the first building one would see on entering the parish of Ketteringham and was intended to reflect the Heveningham's status. In addition, it provided Sir Arthur Heveningham the opportunity to make a point to John Flowerdew who lived at Stanfield Hall.[38] Sir Arthur had a particular dislike of Flowerdew. One of their many falling outs was over access to Wymondham common. High Ash Farmhouse was situated next to the common and provided Sir Arthur the pleasure of showing this part was his.

While in prison at Windsor Castle Sir William wrote in his journal, "Memorandum Concerning the plalting of an acker of wood 1659 presently affeir Mihelmas; on the South west side of a new Fearme House then towardes Windham but in Ketteringham in Norff; where one Good Dayes then Hired Begins: 1 One square ackeir Lying neere this House I First inclosed".[39]

The new farmhouse (Fearme House) towards Windham but in Ketteringham is a reference to High Ash. A scrolled brick on the side of the building has WH on it which is probably a reference to Sir William Heveningham and it is the most obvious of Sir John's eight messuages. Sir William makes reference to the planting of an acre (ackeir) with 250 ashes (arches), might this be the origin of the name High Ash?

Possibly because part of neighbouring Stanfield Hall is in Wymondham it is not always appreciated that is also partly in Ketteringham. Other than Stanfield Hall's North Lodge, which is on St Thomas Lane, Stanfield Hall cannot be seen from Ketteringham. Apart from a few fragments of 16th century brick at the rear, little remains of the house from the Heveningham period.[40]

Notes

1. Dwelling including outbuildings and land.
2. Hunter, *The History and Topography of Ketteringham in the county of Norfolk*, p.43.
3. Calculation based on information in Domesday and applying the formula suggested by Dyer, *Making a living in the Middle Ages*, p.25.
4. Farebrother & Co, Sales Catalogue, p.4.
5. A rood is a quarter of an acre. There are forty perches to a rood.
6. Barringer, *Faden's map of Norfolk*, p.21.
7. Ibid., p.21.
8. Barringer, *Bryant's map of Norfolk in 1826*, p.57.
9. Cattermole ed., *Wymondham Abbey*, p.11.
10. Ibid. 2, p.21.
11. Ibid., P.21.
12. Rackham, *The History of the countryside: The classic history of Britain's landscape, flora and fauna*, p.145.
13. Ibid. 4, p.4.
14. Ibid. 12, p.168.
15. The British Newspaper Archive.
16. Historic England, list entry number 1373140.
17. Wade-Martins ed., *An Historic Atlas of Norfolk*, p.124.
18. Ibid. 16, list entry number 1050571.
19. Sharpe, *Early Modern England*, p.137.
20. localhistories.org entry for Norwich.

21. Ibid. 18, p.41.

22. Ibid. 2, p.66.

23. NRO. MC 107/1.

24. Blomefield, *An Essay Towards A Topographical History of the County of Norfolk:* vol. 5 p.90.

25. Ibid.

26. TNA, prob/11/191.

27. TNA, prob/11/433.

28. Ibid. 2,p.63.

29. Smith, *County and Court: Government and politics in Norfolk 1558-1603,* p.159.

30. Rose, 9515 Ketteringham.

31. Wellgate cottage is now divided into two dwellings.

32. Ibid. 16, list entry number, 1170223.

33. Ibid., list entry number, 1169904.

34. Ibid., list entry number, 1170190.

35. Ibid., list entry number, 1373144.

36. Ibid., list entry number, 1170176.

37. Ibid., list entry number, 1373141.

38. Ibid. 15, p.192.

39. Ibid., 22.

40. Hudson, *Stanfield Hall.*

Richard Haggar

In the last two chapters I considered how the history of Ketteringham was entwined with the history of the Heveninghams and how they were able to make changes to suit their requirements and gradually gain ownership of most of the village. Despite the Heveninghams' increased importance they, like the village, had little control on decisions made, and events that occurred, elsewhere. We have already seen one of these, the English Civil War. That had implications for the villages and a profound impact on the Heveningham family.

During the period of the Heveninghams' another event took place which, from the wider historical perspective, was as monumental as the Civil War and would have implications for the Heveninghams and a profound impact on the villagers. As such I will approach this event from the perspective of someone who would have appreciated this more than anyone.

The Heveninghams may have considered themselves to be the most important people in the village, but for the families of those who worked the land the village priest was the most important. Unlike the Lord of the Manor, who they rarely saw, they saw the priest every Sunday. He baptised every villager into the Christian community, joined couples in marriage, ministered the last rites and smoothed their passage into the next world. He helped the people of Ketteringham make sense of a world that revolved around survival and the fear of ever-present death. The priests' names are recorded and are probably the nearest we can get to the mass of villagers whose names we will never know. Through his eyes and experiences, we may be able to appreciate how national historic events impact upon and write the local history of a small village.

On the south wall of the chancel of St Peter's is a monumental brass to Richard Wright who served as vicar from 1515 to 1520.[1] At this time Sir John Heveningham was the Lord of the Manor and, with his wife Alice, would be buried in the chancel. Richard had been appointed vicar to St Peter's by the Prior of Pentney Priory, Richard Woodbridge. The Priory appropriated St Peter's nearly 400 hundred years earlier. Appropriation had given the Prior the privilege of appointing the resident priest, but he was also responsible for the fabric of the chancel. The parishioners were responsible for the nave.

Richard Wright brass.

The Heveninghams, like the Greys before them, viewed St Peter's as their church and both chose to invest in the church. This included the chancel although this was the responsibility of the Prior. It was likely that the Prior was happy to see the Greys undertake and pay for the work on the church. Having undertaken the work, it is not surprising that there are many references to the family included in the building and particularly the chancel. It is not known who placed the brass in the chancel. The Prior was aware the appropriation lay with him and not at the Hall adjacent. Possibly he felt, despite Richard Wright only being vicar for five years, he needed to place a brass plate to the memory of his vicar. A reminder of who held the advowson. The brass is now positioned close to the Heveningham tomb and under Sir Henry and Lady Jane Grey's brasses although both brasses were originally set in stones near the altar. The only memorial to a vicar prior to Richard Wright was to William Ive who died in 1490 in the time of Sir Henry Grey, possibly making a similar point in the newly refurbished chancel. The tension between those in the Hall and St Peter's has a long history.

Richard Wright belonged to Pentney Priory which was a house of Austin canons who, like the other Austin Friars, followed the rules of St Augustine. The Austin Friars lived a monastic life, the canons lived in the community. As an Austin canon he had taken the three vows of chastity, poverty and obedience.

When Richard Wright died in 1520 the then prior, John Hawe, chose Henry Haggar as vicar. He carried out this role for ten years. We do not know where he was buried, there is no memorial to him in the church. Possibly the new prior, Robert Codde did not feel they still needed to make a point to the Heveninghams as to whose church it was, or maybe the death of John Heveningham in the same year, has overshadowed Haggar's.

When Robert Codde chose Henry's brother Richard Haggar[2] as the next vicar, he could not have known it would be the last he, or anyone else, would choose, not only for Ketteringham, but for any of Pentney's appropriated churches. Robert Codde could not have known the turmoil his Religious House would face, or Richard Haggar the effect on his new parishioners.

We know little of Richard Haggar the person but, from what he was to experience in his lifetime it might suggest he was strong both in character and faith. If strength comes from genes, possibly his Viking heritage helped. His family took their name from their Danish hometown Agard where they originated. Richard, like his brother Henry, had probably attended the almonry school at Pentney Priory. There he spent many years studying and training for the monastic life. At eighteen he became a novice. Rather than becoming a monk he chose to become a member of the secular clergy. He probably visited Ketteringham on many occasions when his brother was vicar. He helped him carry out his duties and was known to the people of Ketteringham. On Henry's death in 1529, Richard was the natural choice to take on the role of vicar and resident priest.

The Prior owned 52 acres of land in Ketteringham and took the income from the more valuable Great Tithes. Richard Haggar was vicar and, as such, had 28 acres of glebe land. After paying 10s 7½d for Synodals and Procurations the vicar's living was £6.[3] This was a poor living. It is not known if he cultivated his 28 acres or leased it out. He, and it would appear his brother before him, was also a tenant of the Priory-lands. There is a record of a rental agreement, dated 24 January 1529, for twenty years at a rent of 100 shillings per annum.[4] With two large landholdings in the village it is likely the vicar managed his landholding leaving cultivating to others giving him greater time to carry out his many duties as a priest. At the Priory's almonry school, he would have learnt his duties as stipulated by Oculus Sacerdotus, 'priest's eye'. He may have been given a copy on leaving the Priory. His involvement in the lives of those in his parish was considerable. He gave instruction on how they should behave and bring up their children. In addition to church services he would visit parishioners in their own homes. With the population of Ketteringham likely greater than it is now and visits being carried out on foot this would consume much of his time. It is not recorded if he had any assistance in his duties and his vow of chastity would limit any help from offspring. Carrying out his duties as priest gave him the opportunity to appreciate the hard life, struggles and concerns of the vast majority of the population of Ketteringham.

The vicarage building (Church Cottage) existed at this time. The rectory we see today (Hall Farmhouse / Pelican House) did not, but an earlier house stood on the site of the present building. Which one did Richard Haggar live in? As an Austin canon one of the main vows was of poverty. Perhaps that and the vow of obedience resulted in him choosing to be close to the church and the convenience of the vicarage. He may not have been given the choice. As vicar he had the vicarage and the rectory was for the rector, the Prior, Robert Codde. The Prior lived at Pentney Priory and if he so wished had many rectories in appropriated parishes Norfolk to choose from. In 1291 the Prior held property in thirty-four parishes in Norfolk.[5] We do not know who lived at Ketteringham's rectory or consequently the purpose it served.

The walls of churches in medieval times were covered in paintings explaining the Christian story to a congregation who could not read or understand the Latin used at the services they regularly attended. The walls of Haggar's St Peter's would have been similarly adorned the pictures, brightly coloured as the church was dark and lit by many candles. This would make the stained glass of the east window appear more pronounced. Here was depicted in glass God the Annunciation, and the Coronation of the

The Rectory today, 2022.

Virgin Mary, flanked by angles saints: St Edmund, John the Baptist, Margaret, Catherine, George, and Michael. The stained glass also includes a depiction of Sir Henry Grey in armour along with the shields of his ancestors. The human face of God in the form of wooden carvings of Jesus and his mother watched over them from the top of the rood screen. This was the Christian family which not only was Richard Haggar part of, but one to which the whole village belonged. It was a family they joined soon after birth when they were baptised. A family that joined couples together in marriage and provided both rituals and comfort at their death and their passage to the heaven shown in the wall paintings. Like a traditional worldly family, they all wanted to be part of it, to be excluded was unthinkable and so they obeyed the rules laid down by those in charge of the family, the clergy, Richard Haggar. Since 1215 people had been required to acknowledge their sins annually to the parish priest and carry out a penance for them before they were allowed to attend Easter Eucharist. Richard would grant absolution, if the wrongdoing was against God this would be put right by the sacrament, if against a neighbour then restitution was decided upon. The paintings on the church walls explained what would happen if they took no action to gain forgiveness from God, a gruesome picture of hell as opposed to the painting of a wondrous heaven. A third place was also shown separating the two, purgatory.

This was a place where those who had died went to be purified before entering heaven. In the early Medieval Period, the church introduced indulgencies as means of reducing time spent in purgatory. Indulgencies took the form of good works, donations or prayer. Although they funded much good work, such as hospitals, by the late Medieval Period they were being seen by some as over commercialised and a means of wealth generation for the church. It is unlikely to have been a concern to those who gathered on Sunday in Ketteringham to see Richard Haggar perform the Eucharist. In 1517 they would have been unaware that a German friar named Martin Luther challenged this practice along with ninety-four other practices of the church. The newly invented printing press, however, allowed Luther's ideas to spread across Europe and Richard might soon have heard of them circulating around England.

Henry VIII was on the throne of England and he did not like these new ideas and Protestantism as it was known. He wrote a pamphlet in support of the Seven Catholic Sacraments criticising Martin Luther's protestant teaching on the subject. The Pope, Leo X, in gratitude for his support, bestowed the honour and title 'Defender of the Faith' on the King. The support of the King from the Pope would not last. The King wanted his marriage to Catherine to be annulled enabling him to marry Anne Boleyn, who he hoped would give him a son. This request was ignored by the Pope which ultimately resulted in Henry breaking with Rome, and in 1534 Parliament passed the Act of Supremacy under which Henry was "the only supreme head on earth of the Church of England".

Having broken with Rome and the Catholic tradition, a reformation of the English church took place. The process of reformation in England was slow and carried out piecemeal during which time priests like Richard Haggar had to face their congregations.

Haggar saw the Pope as the earthly leader of the church. The successor of St Peter whom Jesus had declared would be the 'rock' upon which the church would be built. Richard Haggar's church in Ketteringham was named after St Peter but he now answered to the King not to the Pope. Whether Richard accepted this we will never know, but to question this was made an act of treason in 1534. The people of Ketteringham came to his church and regarded the familiar pictures and carvings of the saints as relations of theirs

Henry VIII.

who lived in a parallel heavenly world: a family who they prayed to and who would listen and help them in the earthly world. There was an altar to St Mary illuminated by candles. To the people of Ketteringham she was a mother just like their mother. How did Richard Haggar explain to his congregation that a law had been passed that forbade these images, and the paintings of the heavenly family of saints that adorned the rood screen were to be defaced? Augustine had been canonised by Pope Boniface VIII and was part of the Christian family of saints probably one who was depicted in Ketteringham Church. How did Richard Haggar come to terms when having lived his life by the rule of St Augustine, it too was destroyed? He may have felt these were dark days for his little church which would not have been helped by a law outlawing all candles except those before the altar. The saints were seen as people who would help them get to heaven: if the saints could not intercede for them how would they be saved? The law now required a bible in every church in England. This might be of interest to the Heveningham family who were able to read. It is doubtful if the villagers were literate. The church warden who was required to sign the glebe terrier of 1613 marked his name with a X. A church registry was required to be kept (Ketteringham's dates from 1685).

It is quite possible that despite the new laws no action was implemented in Henry VIII's reign. Laws do not change the way you think and believe. What the people of Ketteringham thought and believed is not possible to determine, but one early injunction would have upset the villagers, the abolition of many feast days. There are no records of the feast days lost at St Peter's but evidence from Holy Trinity Church, Long Melford, Suffolk, showed that this included the major Rogation festivals held in April and three minor Rogations in the summer. Mid-summer eve bonfire and watching, St Thomas bonfire, feast and watching, Christmas and the following three days of feasts for, St Stephen's choir, St John the Evangelist and on the last day the Feast of the Holy Innocent. People worked hard and any suggestion that they had not the right to celebrate with a feast would not have been well received.

Henry VIII needed money. He was now in charge of the church, the church owned between a fifth and a third of all the land in England much of which belonged to the many Religious Houses. If he could access this land and the wealth of these institutions, he could raise the funds he required. He needed to know how much they were worth and to find a reason to justify taking them over. Henry's chief minister, Thomas Cromwell, who had played an important role in annulling Henry's marriage was a great supporter of the reformation. In 1534 he initiated a visitation of the monasteries, supposedly to check on their character but the real intention was to gauge their wealth. Pentney Priory was visited in 1535 and its annual income, which now included Wormegay, was found to be £170 4s 9 ¾d.[6] A secret visit was made by Legh and Ap Rice early the following year at which the Prior, Robert Codde was found to have "carried out an intrigue with the abbess of Marham".[7] Five canons also confessed to Legh and Rice of having "scandalous lives". These reports have to be seen as part of Cromwell's greater plans for the religious houses. Cromwell received many reports from other establishments referring to immorality which, along with reports of financial irregularities, supplied the justification he required to suppress the monasteries. Richard Haggar knew his Prior was a good man as were his fellow canons. A mere two months later the county commissioners visited Pentney and reported; "the Priory of Chanones of Pentney and Wormegay of the Order of Seynt Augustine' had a clear annual value of £180 19s. 0¾d.; that the religious persons in the house numbered nine, 'alle Prystes of very honest name and goode religious persones who doue desyre the kynges highness to contynue and remayne in religione'; that eighty-three other persons had their living there—namely, twenty-three hinds, thirty household servants, and thirty children and other poor servants; that the lead and bells were worth £180, and that the house was in very good and requisite repair; that the goods were worth £119 5s. 6d.; that the woods were worth £20; and that £16 was owing to the house".[8]

The report from the county commissioners suggests the original evidence against the Prior and his house as false and was indeed part of Cromwell's plan. In 1536, the dissolution of the monasteries began with the Dissolution of the Lesser Monasteries Act coming into force, lesser monasteries were those valued at less than £200. This should have included Pentney Priory but in March of that year Richard Southwell, a county commissioner and Robert Hogen wrote to Cromwell that the; "Prior relieved those quarters wondrously where he dwells, and it would be a pity not to spare a house that feeds so many indigent poor, which is in a good state, maintains good service, and does so many charitable deeds".[9] Further confirmation of the earlier accusations against his character were false.[10]

Many lay people were affected by the Dissolution leading to riots in Northern England. The county commissioners, Townsend, Paston, Southwell and Mildmay visited Pentney on 6 October 1536 and cited these riots in a subsequent report as a reason Pentney had not been suppressed. This, however, was only a delay and on 16 February 1537 the county

Wymondham Abbey, 2001.

commissioners sold to the Lord of Rutland; "alle the stuff in the Quyre for xls. the stuffe in Lady Chappell fo. xs., and the stuffe in the vestry for £13 6s. 8d". He also purchased the contents of the conventual buildings, cattle, corn, hay and growing crops; the total amounting to £114 15s. 9d. In addition to this the plate, in the custody of Richard Southwell, was valued at £22 11s. 4d. The debts of the house amounted to £16.[11]

The now ex-Prior Codde was not only given a pension of £24 but was appointed warden of the hospital of St Giles indicating the respect in which he was held.

From Ketteringham Common the towers of Wymondham Abbey could clearly be seen. Wymondham was the local market town and would be familiar to the villagers. The town was dominated by the Benedictine Abbey and the community it housed. It provided not only the spiritual needs of the town but welfare, education and employment. It consumed large amounts of produce supplied by the surrounding communities including Ketteringham. Reference is made in the early 16th century of faggots being supplied to the abbey from woods including Cromwells Wood and Stanfield Wood both close to and possibly on Ketteringham land. In 1538 Wymondham Abbey was suppressed. The King appointed John Flowerdew as his Sergeant-at-Law and his commissioner at the Dissolution of the Abbey. Flowerdew stayed at nearby Stanfield Hall as he carried out the King's work. The demolition of the abbey buildings must have come as nearly as much of a shock to the people of Ketteringham as it did to those in Wymondham. Like the lands of Pentney, Wymondham Abbey lands were confiscated and sold off. Those who bought this land were interested in financial gain and the income from the local tithes were not returned to the local economy.

Despite the suppression of Pentney Priory it appears Richard Haggar remained vicar at Ketteringham. He had a vicarage, income from glebe lands and a role, so unless asked to leave it made sense to stay, especially as it is likely he had nowhere else to go. He lost the rectory lands but these he had paid rent on and they may not have been of great advantage to him. These lands went to the King and were sold in 1545 to Robert Rumbald (or Reynbold) in return for one sixtieth part of a Knight's fee (worth £4 per annum).[12] Robert Rumbald was a grocer (although described as a merchant at the inquest following his death) from Norwich and brother of a successful and wealthy merchant, William Rumbald based in Ipswich. Robert died in 1558 and his son Benjamin and wife Anne with their daughter and Anne's sister Elizabeth lived in the rectory.

Henry VIII died and his son Edward came to the throne. He was only nine years old and the Duke of Somerset became Lord Protector. Whereas Henry had not been totally committed to Protestantism the Duke of Somerset was a member of the Seymour family who were staunch Protestants. In 1547 images and painting were ordered be removed from churches and walls 'whited'. Pulpits, poor-boxes and chests for registry now had to be provided. Sepulchre and rood lights were no longer allowed. It is likely St Peter's lost its rood screen at this time along with the heads of the saints in the east window. The paintings on the walls were covered over in white. There is evidence of some colour to this day on the font, so it is possible this was left or the removal of the colour was not very thorough. This must have made a dramatic change to the character of the building and to the atmosphere during services. Like the changes made by Edward's father, it is likely that the villages felt the removal of further festivals to be the most resented. Plough Monday celebrations were banned as were wakes and church-ales. Two years later a further change came to the 'atmosphere' of St Peter's when the altar was removed from the east end and replaced by a communion table.

The east window with the heads of the saints removed, 2022.

In the final days of Edward's reign, in 1552 inventories of Norfolk church goods took place. St Peter's inventory is dated 29 August, 1552.[13] It recorded and valued items used as part of religious services which included: vestments, chalice, altar and other cloths, candlesticks and church bells. We do not have an inventory before the reformation so a direct comparison before and after reformation cannot be made. An indication of the effect of the reformation on St Peter's, however, can be detected especially when neighbouring church inventories are considered. In 1538 Henry VIII limited candles in a church to those before an altar. The 1552 inventory records Ketteringham as having two candlesticks which must have been the two that remained in front of the altar. The neighbouring church at Intwood also had two, but Keswick is reduced to one (although Keswick did have a holy water stoup) and Hethersett, Hethel and East Carleton had none at all.[14] Edward's instruction to replace the altar with a communion table can be seen in the record of altar cloths. Ketteringham is recorded as having two altar cloths "erased" (along with two towels, surplice and rochet) leaving it with two altar cloths. Intwood had one but Hethel had two "erased" leaving it without any. Neither Hethersett nor Keswick had an altar cloth. East Carlton had two cloths which were valued but not described as altar cloths, possibly 'make do' altar cloths.

The most valuable item, other than the bells, in these churches was the silver chalice. The stricter laws introduced by Edward in 1547 meant that chalices were melted down or sold. The valuation is by weight of silver. Although Hethersett has neither candlesticks nor altar cloths it had by far the most expensive chalice, valued at 40s 3d (as an item). East Carleton also with no candlesticks or dedicated altar cloths had the third most valuable at 29s 9d.[15] These were probably richly decorated churches prior to the reformation and lost the most. Intwood, despite having two candlesticks and an altar cloth has no chalice. Ketteringham appears to have fared the best locally, having not only two candlesticks, two altar cloths and a chalice valued at 35s 7d.[16]

The valuation document may also give another insight into Richard Haggar. The document was signed not only by Richard but also by Thomas Haggar. Was it a coincidence that both shared the same surname or was Thomas, Richard Haggar's son? Priests were allowed to marry in 1549 but that would make Thomas but three years old. He may therefore have had an extended family living nearby with whom he could share his troubles during this period of change.

Richard Haggar did not only have to deal with disruption from the actions of the monarchy during his time at Ketteringham, an event now called, Kett's Rebellion also occurred while he was vicar. There are no written accounts of involvement by people of Ketteringham in this rebellion, although it is very likely that underlying discontent at the root of the uprising would have been shared by them.

The importance of common land has been mentioned previously. The large common that covered the heavy lands between Hethersett, Ketteringham,

Wymondham and Great Melton was gradually being enclosed. This was not an illegal act as the common land was invariably owned by the Lord of the Manor and if he left sufficient for those with commoners' rights, it was acceptable in law. The reduction in the amount of common land made it harder for those who depended on the use of this additional land to make their farms viable. In Norfolk, riots broke out against further enclosure at Fakenham in 1520 and 1525. Ten miles west of Ketteringham, Hingham experienced riots in 1539 over Sir Henry Parker enclosing some of their common. Revolts were also happening in other parts of England fuelled by the same concerns but it would be the rebellion that started in Wymondham which would make the greatest impact and its leader who would be remembered.

The enclosure of common land was not the only cause of discontent. At the dissolution of the monasteries the lands of the religious houses were sold off. Members of the gentry brought the land for the purpose of making money. The country was growing wealthy on the production of wool and this land was turned over to sheep grazing. The rich became wealthier and the loss of the commons made the poor more so. Growing wealth disparity tends to unsettle a society. The rearing of sheep required fewer workers and unemployment grew. Prices rose 30% between 1530 and 1549. Unemployed workers who were forced to beg could face punishment. An Act of Parliament in 1536 ordered whipping for all unlicensed beggars for the first offence, mutilation for the second and hanging for the third.[17] The monasteries that might once have helped the poor were no more.

A rising began at nearby Attleborough on 20 June 1549. John Green, Lord of the Manor of Wilby, fenced off and planted hedges around the common land belonging to his manor. These were knocked down by the local inhabitants. A little over two weeks later, on 6 July 1549, the annual festival celebrating Thomas a' Becket's appointment as Archbishop of Canterbury took place. This was a major two-day event attended by many from the surrounding area. Here people would have had the chance to meet and converse. Their state of poverty and the lack of concern of the landowners would have been a major gripe they all shared. The events less than seven miles down the road in Attleborough would have been a major talking point. No doubt many saw justification in the action taken by the locals. The local precedence had been set. The Monday after the weekend fair ended fences at nearby Morley were pulled down. The group then moved to Hethersett to tear down fences belonging to John Flowerdew who was enclosing part of Wymondham Common. Whether folk from Ketteringham were involved we do not know, but they were likely very sympathetic.

John Flowerdew had been appointed by Henry VIII as his Sergeant-at-Law and was his commissioner at the Dissolution. He stayed at Stanfield Hall while acting on behalf of the King as the Abbey was broken up. The people of Wymondham had already used part of the Abbey as a church and were given permission by the church to continue to do so. They wished to extend this building using materials from the Abbey buildings. Although the King supported the towns folk in this venture, it appears his commissioner did not. Flowerdew chose not to give them the lead they had paid for. This would not have been forgotten as they tore down his new fences on Wymondham Common. Attack being the best form of defence, combined with a bribe of 40d (17p), he tried to turn the angry group against another landowner carrying out similar enclosure across the common on the Wymondham side, Robert Kett. Robert Kett was a local tanner and yeoman farmer who, educated at the Abbey, had attempted to save much of the Abbey's fabric and consequently neither were fond of each other. When the group sent by Flowerdew arrived at Kett's enclosure Robert gave them a hand to remove his fencing saying, "Whatever lands I have enclosed shall be made common unto ye and all men, and my own hand shall first perform it".[18] Robert Kett then led the men back to Hethersett where they demolished Flowerdew's fences. The disgruntled men had found a leader in their fight against enclosures.

The following day, 9 July, Robert Kett and his followers assembled at an oak tree on Wymondham common and agreed to march to Norwich on the next day. On the march they were joined by other rebels. Attempts were made to make them return home, but they made camp outside Norwich on Mousehold Heath three days later. Here they stayed for nearly seven weeks. By 20 July the camp may have numbered 10,000. They formed their own government where each of the 24 Hundreds present sent two representatives. Ketteringham like Hethersett is in the Hundred of Humbleyard. The rebels issued their grievances in a document known as 'The twenty-nine requests' which apart from concern over enclosures and the problems of poor farmers also included an array of other concerns. A Royal Herald was sent to the camp to offer those on Mousehold a royal pardon and asked them to disperse. Kett's reply was: "Kings and princes are want to pardon wicked persons not innocent and just men. We ... have deserved nothing and are guilty ourselves of no crime".[19]

He rejected the pardon. The Herald returned to Norwich and guards were positioned at the city gates with special attention paid to reinforcing Bishopgate Bridge which faced Mousehold Heath. Here the two sides met and fought. Despite the use of cannon and archers, the rebels' superior numbers led to the city surrendering to Kett's men. The Herald offered another pardon which again was rejected.

A royal army was raised and dispatched to Norwich. The rebels had returned to Mousehold and the army under the Earl of Northampton set up base in the city. That night the rebels attacked the city but failed to take it. The following day the rebels attacked again this time taking the city. A second royal army was prepared under John Dudley, the Earl of Warwick. This was a much larger and better equipped army than the previous one. Before entering the city Warwick was entertained by Sir Thomas Gresham at Intwood Hall. Kett sent out a delegation from Norwich's St Stephens Gate to ask for pardon for the rebels, not including Kett. This was being discussed and may have been accepted if a young boy had not turned to face the Royal Herald and bared his bottom. This upset the Herald's bodyguard who shot the boy dead. The turmoil that resulted brought negotiations to an end. Warwick attacked the city and the rebels fled back to Mousehold. Following a failed attempt to retake the city and with dwindling supplies, the rebels left their camp at Mousehold. Under cover of darkness, they moved to Dussindale where they made defensive arrangements for a predicted battle. Kett's band of rebels was no match for Warwick's trained soldiers. When they met, Warwick lost 200 men while the rebels lost 3,000. The rebellion was over. Following the battle some rebels were executed. Shortly after Robert Kett was arrested, both he and his brother William were sent to the Tower of London. Both were found guilty of treason, William was hanged in Wymondham from the west tower of the abbey church, Robert from Norwich Castle where he was left hanging as an example to would-be rebels. Nearly 4,000 died in the rebellion of which only 350 were on the government's side.

In his book Hunter indirectly asks the question of Ketteringham's involvement in Kett's Rebellion writing, "It must be considered a remarkable circumstance, that the name Sir Anthony Heveningham never occurs in the printed narrative of this affair".[20] His father's inquest had shown that the majority of Ketteringham's common had already been enclosed. What remained was 40 acres of heath. This might suggest Sir Anthony was not involved in enclosing common land at this time. It is possible that although having sympathy for the rebels' cause, the folk of Ketteringham were not involved. As tenant farmers the risk of losing their livelihood might have been too great a sacrifice for a cause. Richard Haggar would have been grateful for not having to deal with a villager's death. He was a priest of the Church of England with the King as its head. Kett was executed for treason, a crime against the King, and any rebels who supported him also committed treason. Haggar's church was the Heveningham's church and, as gentry, they were unlikely to have any sympathy for those limiting their control on common land they owned. The enclosures continued and were enforced by an Act of Parliament which made organised opposition to enclosures a treasonable offence.

John Dudley, the Duke of Northumberland used the revolt as a means to remove the Duke of Somerset having him executed on a flimsy charge of treason. He was then able to dominate the young King Edward VI. The King was a sickly child, so John Dudley took precautions to protect his position should he die. If Edward died the next in line was Mary Tudor, daughter of Henry VIII's first wife Catherine of Aragon. She was a Catholic who would not tolerate a protestant like John Dudley. Henry VIII's younger sister Mary was Duchess of Suffolk. Dudley married his son Guildford Dudley to the duchess's granddaughter Lady Jane and convinced the King and Privy Council to nominate her as queen before he died. Mary Tudor told the Council she was the rightful Queen and headed for London with her supporters. The Privy changed its allegiance and Mary became queen. The Duke of Northumberland was executed. Lady Jane Grey was Queen for just nine days. Both Lady Jane and her young husband were also executed. There is a piece of folklore in Ketteringham that says, Lady Jane Grey was baptised in the font of St Peter's. If it had been true and Henry Haggar had carried out the baptism, then he would have felt rewarded for all that he had had to endure but it is not the case. The story may have arisen because on the south wall of the chancel is a brass to Lady Jane Grey, however, this is the wife of Sir Henry Grey of Ketteringham not Sir Henry Grey 1st Duke of Suffolk. The Greys had held Ketteringham manor but on Sir Henry Grey's death in 1492 he left the manor to Thomas Heveningham and his wife Anne. Lady Jane was born in about 1537 forty-five years after the manor had passed to the Heveninghams'.

Mary Tudor was a Catholic and married to Philip II of Catholic Spain and, not surprisingly, attempted to turn England's religion back to Catholicism. Rood screens and altars were restored, English books were burnt, procession festivals returned and Papal authority restored. There was a greater fondness for Mary than Somerset and the 'Kett killing' Northumberland. Possibly some in Ketteringham felt this was a return to familiarity. How much did return is not known. There are not any records to show whether a rood screen was put back. It seems improbable that the walls were repainted with their medieval artwork. Five years later, in 1558, Elizabeth, daughter of Anne Boleyn, became Queen Elizabeth I and Protestantism was back. Rood screens and lofts were pulled down, altars removed and the Book of Common Prayer reintroduced. Poor Richard Haggar died in the November 1558 and was buried in Ketteringham's Protestant church. His immediate replacement is not recorded.

Notes

1. Blomefield, *An Essay Towards A Topographical History of the County of Norfolk: vol. 5* p.90.
2. Blomefield spells Haggar with an 'e', Hagger. I have taken the spelling from the earliest written account of the name in a church inventory of 1543. Hunter, *The History and Topography of Ketteringham in the county of Norfolk*, p.59.
3. Ibid., p.89.
4. Hunter, *The History and Topography of Ketteringham in the county of Norfolk*, p.58.
5. British History online.
6. Ibid.
7. Ibid.
8. Ibid.
9. Ibid.
10. Ibid.
11. Ibid.
12. Ibid. 1, p.90.
13. *Norfolk Archaeology* vol. XXXI part II, 1955, p.260.

14. Ibid., p.259.
15. Ibid., p.254.
16. Ibid., p.255.
17. Clayton, *Robert Kett and the Norfolk Rising*, p.19.
18. Hoare, *An Unlikely Rebel: Robert Kett and the Norfolk Rising, 1549*, p.23-5.
19. Ibid, p.39.
20. Ibid. 1, p.45.

The Atkyns Family

This book started with Lady Mary receiving the news of the death of her husband Sir William Heveningham and her fears of the consequences for the estate. She did keep the estate and it remained with the Heveningham until her granddaughter, Abigail's husband sold the estate in 1717. There is an interesting connection between the Heveningham's and the new purchaser.

Sir William Heveningham had died while imprisoned in Windsor Castle. He was one of twenty-eight regicides who, on 8 October 1660, appeared at Clerkenwell before presiding judge Bridgeman all charged with high treason. With Bridgeman were ten other judges. In the south transit of Westminster Abbey is a monument erected to one of these ten judges, Sir Edward Atkyns. In the chancel of St Peter's, Ketteringham is a very similar monument to the same Sir Edward Atkyns. The opening inscription on both Atkyns monuments are the same:

Sir Edward Atkyns memorial, Westminster Abbey.

> To the memory of Sir Edward Atkyns one of the Barons of the Exchequer in the reigns of King Charles the first and second; He was a person of such integrity that he resisted the many advantages and honours offered him by the chiefs of the grand Rebellion. He departed this life in 1669 aged 82 years.

Sir William attended the trial of the King, Sir Edward attended the trial of those who tried the King. Both had found the accused guilty. Both are remembered in the chancel of St Peter's.

Sir Edward Atkyns' first wife Ursula gave him two sons, Robert and Edward, both of whom also became eminent judges. There had been lawyers in the Atkyns family for two hundred years and they had clearly prospered from the profession both financially and by increased standing in society.

Monument to Sir Edward Atkyns, St Peter's Church, Ketteringham.

As well as there being a family tradition that the sons would go into the legal profession, there was a tradition of naming one son, normally the second, Edward which can be confusing.

Edward Atkyns, grandson of the regicide judge Sir Edward Atkyns bought the Ketteringham Estate in 1717 from Henry Heron and Abigail, Sir William Heveningham's granddaughter. Edward's wish to make Ketteringham his family seat is seen in the memorial to his family in St Peter's. This was more than pride in the family's achievements, it was a declaration of the importance and status of the new owners. They may well have hung family portraits on the walls of Ketteringham Hall, but these would have only been seen by those invited to visit the Hall. By placing the memorials in the church, it could be seen by all including the villagers who worshipped every Sunday. The inclusion of earlier generations of the family was designed to create an impression of an established family seat. This was not dissimilar to the burial mounds placed at Five Ways four thousand years earlier which were a declaration that it was the land of our ancestors. The memorial in the church refers to his service to King Charles I and an Atkyns being created Knight of the Bath at the Coronation of Charles II; a statement to distance the family from the previous owner's part in the regicide. The family's loyalty to the monarch is also evident on both of the memorials which states of Edward's (purchaser) father:

> Sir Edward Atkyns… Lord Chief of the Exchequer, which office he discharged with great honour and integrity, but retired at the Revolution from public business to his seat in Norfolk.

The Revolution it refers to is now commonly known as the Glorious Revolution. James II had become King in 1685 and although he did so with the support of Parliament, he was a Catholic. His two daughters, Mary and Anne, were Protestants. It was felt that the King intended to reinstate Catholicism as the nation's religion. This, and concerns that he was not listening to Parliament, led Parliament to 'invite' William of Orange, who had married Mary, to become King and Queen. William landed in Torbay with an army of fifteen thousand. King James offered little resistance and many of his supporters changed side: James fled to France. Parliament met to pass The Bill of Rights. This declared that James had abdicated, that William was now King and Mary Queen, it reasserted the power of Parliament and limited the power of the Crown. In addition, it barred Catholics from the throne thus enshrining in law Protestantism as the nation's religion. When William became King William III in 1689, Sir Edward Atkyns refused to take the oath of allegiance to the new

William III landing at Brixham, Torbay, 5 November 1688 by Jan Wyck.

King and had to resign from his position of Chief Baron of the Exchequer to be replaced by his brother Sir Robert Atkyns. Sir Edward retired to his seat in South Pickenham, Norfolk.

Having purchased the Ketteringham Estate Edward extended its land holding when, in 1743, he purchased nearby Hethersett Cromwells Manor. Apart from this, little is known of his time at the Hall. He did present Samuel Clark AM as vicar in 1728. The Rev. Clark also became vicar of East Dereham in 1741 along with the chapel at Hoe, having become rector in 1740.[1] The reason for Samuel Clark taking on a second parish is not clear but may be a reflection on Ketteringham being a poor living and consequently a need, or desire, for additional income. This was a common practice at the time known as plurality.

Edward Atkyns died in 1750. The Ketteringham Estate passed to his great nephew also Edward Atkyns. He had broken with the age-old tradition of the Atkyns' sons going into law and was a Hamburg merchant. On his death, in 1765, the estate went to his son, yet another Edward, who married Charlotte Walpole in 1779 and had an only child, Wright Edward Atkyns.

During the time of the Heveninghams, much of the Medieval structure and practices in Ketteringham had been replaced. In some cases it was simply no longer relevant, in others it was not convenient for those who lived at the Hall.

To the south of Ketteringham is Hethel. In the Domesday Survey Hethel (Hethella—Heather Hill) had one main manor which, like that of Ketteringham, passed from the Saxon thegn, Ulf to the Norman, Bigod. By the 17th century Hethel too was an estate dominated by its Hall. When sold in 1820, the sale catalogue described Hethel Hall as being of moderate size with 14 rooms and an estate consisting of approximately 1730 acres.[2]

When the Heveninghams owned Ketteringham Hall, Hethel Hall was owned by the Branthwayts, a family with a long pedigree of producing eminent lawyers. They, like the Heveninghams, placed great importance on marrying between the 'better' families. This had, however, not stopped Arthur Branthwayt's daughter Elizabeth eloping and marrying Thomas Beevor, the son of a Norwich brewer. This resulted in Elizabeth's husband, Thomas Beevor becoming Squire of Hethel Hall in 1752. Any concerns about Thomas Beevor's lowly status were rectified in 1784 when Thomas was created a baronet for his services to agriculture.[3]

In January, 1789 Sir Thomas Beevor (as he had become), Thomas Beevor (his son and heir) and Randall Burroughes, all three Justices of the Peace, met at Hethel Hall. During the meeting concerns were expressed that, in order to travel from Carlton Common to Hethersett, they had to pass through Ketteringham Park and the highway, which was considered to be "narrow and cannot be conveniently enlarged and made commodious for travellers".[4] To overcome these limitations it was proposed to build a new highway, across Atkyns' land, from the Blacksmith's in East Carlton to Five Ways (modern day Hethersett Road) bypassing Ketteringham Park altogether. The proposal reserved for "Thomas Beevor and his heirs and other inhabitants in occupation of Hethel Hall a free passage...of the said old highway".[5] (That is through Ketteringham Park). Edward Atkyns did not attend the meeting, for reasons that will become apparent, but sent his agent, John Futter, who placed his seal in agreement to the proposal on his behalf. This agreement received its official approval three years later and was placed with the Clerk of the Peace for Norfolk.

The reason for the closure of one highway and the construction of another was justified on the grounds that the old highway was inadequate and could not be improved. It is surprising that the existing highway across Mr Atkyns' land, most of which was open parkland, could not accommodate any widening and therefore the only solution was to build a new highway across farmland. After all, apart from the effort and cost of a new highway, the highway would reduce farm estate income. The reason given suggests an attempt to gain official approval for improvements to the Ketteringham Estate. The insertion of a clause in the agreement that maintained the legal right of way for those at Hethel Hall to use the old route, suggests Mr Atkyns was the instigator and this was a 'sweetener' to obtain Sir Thomas Beevor's

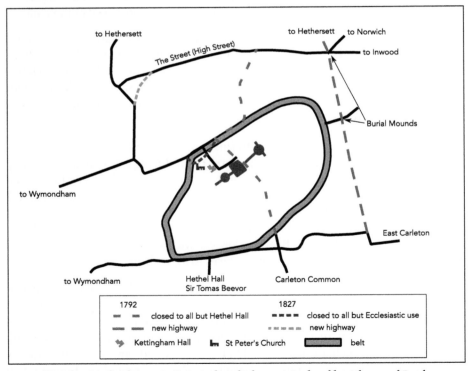

Map showing the changes to Ketteringham highways introduced by Atkyns and Peach.

approval. Sir Thomas' son, Miles, was an ordained minister and, in addition to Hethel, vicar of St Peter's. The use of the old route through Ketteringham Park would be much shorter than the new highway. Owen Chadwick writes of Rev. Dr Miles Beevor, "he came to Ketteringham only to perform his duties. If he found no congregation waiting, he locked the church and rode home, uncomplaining".[6] Knowing he could cut through Ketteringham Park would have pleased him.

The paths which crossed the three great open fields in medieval times allowed the villagers to access both their strips and the common. The old and new highway are described as "leading from Carlton Common". The old highway was once known as Over Gate (Gata) Way. This ran by the Hall across the Street or Gata (High Street) towards Hethersett and possibly separated the two great fields called Hethersett and Carlton. The Heveninghams had landscaped the park and edged it with a belt of trees to screen and frame the parkland. Edward Atkyns now wanted the park to be a more private location, limiting access to others where possible. These roads across the park remain private to this day.

Along with the old ways across the lord's land, the last connection the estate had with the common finally disappeared. When the Atkyns' sold the estate in 1837, there was no mention of any common in Ketteringham. The large expanse of medieval common that stretched between Wymondham and Hethersett and of which it was once part, was vastly reduced in size as a result of hundreds of years of nibbling at its edge and drainage. The final loss was the result of Parliamentary enclosures.

Parliamentary enclosures occurred in two phases. The first happened in the 1760s and 1780s. The second took place during the time of the French Revolution and the Napoleonic War, between 1793 and 1815. The latter was the period of the greater enclosure in Norfolk. Ketteringham parish was unusual in having lost all but 40 acres of common and was not affected by Parliamentary enclosure. However, the Ketteringham Estate was. In 1810, an Act was passed for the enclosure of the parish of Wymondham.[7] Within the enclosure settlement was a plot of land awarded to Charlotte Atkyns. This was on the Wymondham side of the parish boundary on High Ash Road. The enclosed land became part of one of the estate's farms in East Carleton (White Gates) and was not surprisingly, known as 'common piece' (sharing its name with the enclosure leading off the High Street). The great common was carved up into regular rectangular fields.

Ketteringham Common had largely disappeared during the time of the Heveninghams. The large expanse of former common to the south of Smeeth Wood had become grazing because wool was a profitable commodity. The price of wool had increased fourfold between 1500 to 1640. From 1640 prices started to fall and continued to do so for the next hundred years.[8] Livestock prices had shown a consistent rise between 1500 and 1750. Livestock includes sheep, cattle, pigs, horses, poultry and rabbits. It is not clear if the Heveninghams enclosed the former common open grazing land for cattle and planted grain to achieve a better return than wool. It may have been a piecemeal approach with some arable enclosures created where the land best suited a grain crop while others were enclosed for cattle grazing and the remainder left open grazing for sheep.

If the enclosure of the grazing was not completed under the Heveninghams, it was during the time of the Atkyns. When the Atkyns sold the Estate in 1837 the catalogue lists each of the new enclosures on the grazing land by the functional name derived by the acreage. It gives the use of each enclosure and the income it provides. Of those so described, 228.5 acres are described as arable and only 58.5 pasture, just 20% of the total. At the time horses were used to work the land and for transport. There is an additional 37 acres described as horse pasture. The total arable for the estate exceeds 1145 acres with less than 300 acres recorded as pasture. Three-quarters of the farmed land in Ketteringham alone was arable. This is not surprising at a time of high grain prices, the result of the Napoleonic War, a growing population and a number of bad harvests. In addition, between 1815-1846, the Corn Laws were in force. These restricted imports of grain which kept prices high for the benefit of domestic producers.

The 1837 sale catalogue lists the buildings belonging to farms. Three of the eight farms are described as having a turnip house. The turnip was a root crop introduced as part of the Norfolk four-course rotation. The system involves a cycle of planting wheat, turnips, barley, clover and /or grasses which produced more grazing and fodder in the form of turnips. The result was fatter livestock and more manure to fertilize the fields. Along with turnip houses, cattle and bullock lodges are recorded indicating that cattle played an important part in the agricultural economy.

The other former piece of the medieval common, Smeeth Wood had no recorded commoners' rights. It could supply timber as required and was used as a source of income especially, as in Charlotte Atkyns' case, when times were hard. The woods also provided areas for hunting and were described, when the estate was sold as "forming fine preserves for game". In addition to Smeeth Wood, Ketteringham had other woods. The largest was the former deer park, Park Wood, at 21.5 acres. The three Belts, created to make the park surrounding the Hall private, formed further woodland. The Belt in Ketteringham was 11 acres and that which extended into the Parish of East Carlton was 4 acres. A further 3 acre belt formed the northern boundary of the parkland. Although the role of these woods was to enhance the landscape surrounding the Hall, they were also managed, The Belt was coppiced and Park Wood provided standing timber, both of which are still managed this way today. The field between Park Wood and The Belt was recorded, when the Atkyns' sold the Estate, as Stump Park. It is likely that this field of nearly 6 acres was felled to provide the controversial sale of oak and ash in April 1823. The Boileaus later chose to keep this field as open pasture and it was not until the 20th century that it reverted back to woodland and it is now managed in conjunction with Park Wood. When the Atkyns left the Hall there was just over 132 acres of woodland although, apart from the above, it was described as plantation; its main purpose was the growing of trees for wood and timber for local use or as a commercial crop. Most were small clumps of trees, in the corner of enclosures of less than an acre. Some still exist but others were lost as small enclosures were combined with neighbouring ones.

Ketteringham's common, like open field farming, had disappeared but some remnants of the village's medieval land use remained. St Peter's still retained its glebe land in the parish. In 1792 Rev. Miles Beevor, vicar of St Peter's, consolidated his glebe lands. He exchanged twenty pieces of land totalling 29 acres and 35 perches and the redundant parsonage house and grounds for two pieces totalling 32 acres and 32 perches.[9] Those 29 acres of land were in 22 pieces suggesting that they were the remnants of the former acre strips that once formed part of the open fields. Having purchased the estate Sir John Boileau had the legality of this exchange verified in 1839 as the 1792 transfer appeared to be invalid. The investigation described the small pieces of land as,"lying dispersed within the... Parish of Ketteringham".[10] This gives support to the suggestion that these were the original strips of land from the great medieval fields.

Although medieval farming had been superseded, a remnant of the medieval feudal system was still evident in a notice published in the *Norfolk Chronicle* announcing a meeting of the Hethersett General Courts Baron of Charlotte Atkyns on 11 December 1818 for the manor of Hethersett Cromwells, Hethersett Hacons, Hethersett Woodhall and Ketteringham cum Castlings.

> All persons concerned are desired to attend, particularly such tenants who owe suit and service at the said courts, are required to appear and pay their respective quit-rents due and in arrears.[11]

It would appear that the General Courts Baron met every ten years as the *Norfolk Chronicle* featured a notice that:

> The meeting for the manor of Hethersett Cromwells, Hethersett Hacons, Hethersett Woodhall and Ketteringham cum Castlings would be at the King's Head (Public House) Hethersett on 27 October, 1829.[12]

Under feudal law, quit rent was paid as an alternative to feudal obligations. As feudal service had disappeared, quit rent had become a land tax paid to the higher landowner.

Investments were made in Ketteringham Hall. A walled kitchen garden was built behind the Hall with a gardener's cottage of unusual octagonal design.[13] One wall of the garden formed the boundary with the churchyard in which a private entrance connecting the garden to the churchyard was made. It is quite possible

The walled garden looking towards the hall, 2006.

that this was a more elaborate entrance replacing an earlier entrance route from the Hall. The connection between Hall and church continued under the Atkyns. Edwin Rose has dated the iron tie that crosses the chancel to 1769 and that the three buttresses were made from bricks dating to before the 1780s.[14] Edwin Rose comments that, "this suggests that in contrast to many churches, those in authority were concerned to keep the church in good repair at this time". Edward Atkyns was only 11 when he inherited the estate in 1765, so it is not clear who the patron was investing in the church. The Park which now excluded all but invited guests had estate fencing placed around it.

The estate was doing well when in 1794 Edward Atkyns died at only 36 and their son, in 1804, at a mere 24. Charlotte Atkyns erected a fine memorial to them both in the church but there are no 19th century memorials to Charlotte herself. There are monuments from this time, but they refer to Mary who was Edward Atkyns's daughter, who died in 1765. She married her first cousin John Thomas Atkyns and had several children. The boys died young and one of the daughters married General Palmer, the other, Harriot, married Nathaniel William Peach. Nathaniel Peach has a monument but there are none following this until, on the purchase of the estate in 1836 the new owners, the Boileaus, place their monuments in the church. Joseph Hunter, in The History and Topography of Ketteringham, only mentions Charlotte once with reference to her being the wife of Edward Atkyns and mother of Wright Edward. The reason for her near absence from the history at this time is an interesting one.

The Atkyns family was a successful and respected family. The family seat of this branch of the family was now at Ketteringham but their work in the legal profession and later as merchants resulted in much of their time being spent in London. In London families of their status would relax, or go to be seen, at the opera and theatre. The young Edward Atkyns would sometimes go to the Theatre Royal in Drury Lane. Here he saw an actress, Charlotte Walpole, who he fell in love with and married at St James Church, London in the summer of 1779 both aged just 21. Acting was a lowly profession and therefore not considered a suitable occupation for the wife of a member of Atkyns family. Her lack of acceptability would go some way to explain the absence from the memorials, but this is not the only, or possibly the main, reason. It is more likely due to her bankrupting the Ketteringham Estate. Charlotte's absence from the 19th century written history is more than made up for by books written in the 20th which describe how she achieved this: *A Friend of Marie-Antoinette (Lady Atkyns)*, by Frederic Barbey, Chapman & Hall, 1905 and *Mrs "Pimpernel" Atkyns* by E.E.P. Tisdall, 1965.

Whether for a retired actress, having her story told on stage would have brought amusement we will never be known, but a Victoire Sardou's stage play, *Pamela, marchande de frivolites* would be performed in 1896, 30 years after her death.

A year after Edward and Charlotte married, their first, and what would be their only child, Wright Edward was born. He was baptised in Westminster. London appears to be where they chose to spend most of their time Ketteringham being a little too quiet for the young couple. They left Ketteringham Hall in 1784 and moved to France, it has been suggested to avoid creditors. They appear not to have been popular with some in Ketteringham as the *Norfolk Chronicle*, a few years later, in October 1786 reported that someone "wickedly and maliciously put eleven oak stakes and cover them with bushes before one of the Park gates of Mrs Atkyns, of Ketteringham Hall".[15] In France they lived in Lille and began to move in court circles at Versailles.

Back in England, Norwich had been overtaken by Bristol as the second city of England. Bristol thrived on the slave trade, Norwich on trade with the Continent largely based on cloth and silks. Edward Atkyns was a Hamburg merchant making his money from trade with the Continent. In 1787 political instability started to take hold in France. The uncertainty this created would have caused interest, if not concern, amongst the merchants and traders of Norwich. In 1789 the people of Paris stormed and seized The Bastille and popular unrest spread across France; the revolt had turned into what we now know as the French Revolution. Any concern about what was now happening in France must have caused worry for the merchants of Norwich but others in the city celebrated. Norwich had a large community of Non-conformists or Dissenters and they saw it as a victory in the

The Storming of the Bastille, 14 July 1789.

fight for freedom which they hoped would then spread to England.[16] They wore French Revolutionary dress and lit bonfires in the streets and at the market. The ruling class of Britain became concerned as the revolution became ever more violent. Edward and Charlotte Atkyns were in France as it was taking place but rather than fleeing back to England, Charlotte chose to stay in France.

How Charlotte fared during this first stage of the revolution in France is not clear. She left in 1791 and returned to Ketteringham but kept in contact with emigrés of the Revolution. The Revolution resulted in the execution of the King, Louis XVI in January 1793. Charlotte returned to France in the summer of that year. On this visit she met Marie-Antoinette in the Conciergerie. The queen asked if Charlotte would look after her son Louis Charles, the Dauphin. This request became the main objective in Charlotte's life from then on. On 27 March the following year Edward Atkyns died at Ketteringham giving Charlotte greater freedom to pursue her objective.

Marie-Antoinette and family were locked up in Temple prison. Her son Louis Charles was eight. On 3 July 1793 he was given to a cobbler to be brought up to be sympathetic to the revolution. Marie-Antoinette was executed on the 16 October. When the wife of the shoemaker died, it is said the boy was put in a cage and fed through the bars. In 1795 he died, reportedly of scrofula and was buried in a mass grave with no stone. The opportunities in this story to suggest that the Dauphin did not die but escaped are many. One surrounds Ketteringham's Charlotte Atkyns.

Frederic Barbey's book gives his interpretation of Charlotte's attempts which relies on papers placed by Charlotte with her notary in Paris and later given to Barbey. These papers have since gone missing making it difficult to ascertain whether they were genuine. Charlotte Atkyns was genuine in her desire to help Marie-Antoinette and her son escape. This was acknowledged by the memorial placed in St Peter's in 1910. This reads "she was the friend of Marie Antoinette and made several brave attempts to rescue her from prison, and after that Queen's death strove to save the Dauphin of France".

Louis Charles.

When a French King died, it was customary to remove and preserve his heart. In 2000, a DNA test was carried out on the heart confirming Louis Charles, the Dauphin had died in prison. In 2004 his heart was buried next to his parents.[17] Charlotte had been the victim of fraud.

The financial cost of Charlotte Atkyns' support of the French Royalists was great and paid for from the Ketteringham Estate. In 1795, the year the Dauphin died, an advertisement appeared in the *Norfolk Chronicle* announcing the auction of 'fine household furniture, of Mrs. Atkyns at Ketteringham Hall'.[18] This included the contents of the drawing room and carpets, bedding and even the wine from her cellar. Edward and Charlotte Atkyns' son, Wright Edwards, on his father's death in 1794 inherited the Ketteringham Estate. He was just 14 and his mother likely had control of the Estate's financial affairs. This allowed her to continue to pay the ever-increasing costs of

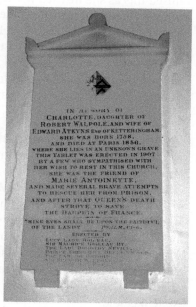

Charlotte's memorial in St Peter's Ketteringham.

her French venture. In 1799 Ketteringham Hall was mortgaged. Her situation was not improved by a major fire during renovations at Ketteringham Hall in 1806. Wright Edwards died in 1804. He was unmarried and, in his will, he left the estate "unto my dear mother Charlotte Atkyns" and after her death "the property to my family". The will was not unusual and would not have been controversial if his mother was not deep in debt with creditors desperate to be paid. In 1809 John

Atkyns Wright, who had married Edward's sister Mary, took Charlotte to the High Court in an attempt to obtain £1000 she owed to his wife. As Wright Edward had left the Ketteringham Estate to his mother, he felt she should sell it to pay her debt. The Master of the Rolls found in John Atkyns Wright's favour but that Wright Edwards' will had only made her a tenant for life and so the estate could be sold. An injunction was also issued to stop her cutting down timber of the estate. It was argued that, as part of the Estate, the value of the timber should be passed to the family as she was only a tenant. On appeal to the House of Lords the verdict was reversed.

In 1810 the people of Britain celebrated the golden jubilee of King George III. As part of Ketteringham's celebrations, Charlotte chose to plant an oak tree. In 1814 the Bourbons were returned to the throne of France and Louis XVIII became King. Charlotte asked for financial recompense of between £30,000 and £40,000 for the costs she incurred in her support for the royal family. The French government refused this as she insisted her claim was for the 'rescue' of Louis XVII. With no money forthcoming from this potential source, she continued to extract as much as she could from the Ketteringham Estate. In 1822 John Atkyns Wright died leaving his share of the Ketteringham estate to his sister Mary and the case returned to court to determine whether Charlotte could take money out of the estate by cutting down timber. In 1823 the court found in favour of Charlotte, giving her the right to cut and sell the timber to repay the debt owed to Thomas Berney Trench and Elizabeth Berney of Morton Hall.

An advertisement appeared in the *Norfolk Chronicle*, "14th April sale by private contract of Oak and Ash standing trees in Ketteringham Wood". Ketteringham Wood was how Smeeth Wood was described on Bryant's contemporary map of 1826. The following month, 10 May 1823, another timber auction was advertised for "Timber Merchants, Ship builders and tanners" (tanners used oak in their craft). This timber was possibly taken from, Inner Park Wood. Later that year, on 17 November 1823 yet another auction at Ketteringham appeared in the *Norfolk Chronicle*, "of pollard Ash, Elm, beech and fir timber". The reference to beech suggests these might be parkland trees, possibly from an area of land that separated Inner Park Wood from the belt giving it the name Stump Park when the Estate was sold.

With assets dwindling and the problem of debt unresolved, in 1824 Charlotte made over the Ketteringham Estate to her sister-in-law Mary Atkyns in return for an annuity. Charlotte's mother died two years later and Charlotte moved to Paris leaving Ketteringham Hall for what would be the last time. She did not, however, break all ties with Ketteringham. In 1829 she supported the opening of the first public day school in the parish at which ten boys and twenty-seven girls attended.[19] In 1836 she died in Paris where she was buried in an unmarked grave.

Mary married Nathaniel Peach in 1824 but died the following year leaving the Estate to her husband. Nathaniel Peach was from one of the leading clothier families of the Stroud Valley. The Ketteringham Estate gave him the opportunity to stand as an MP. He was asked to stand for Norwich in 1826 but declined the offer. He acquired property in Dorset and became MP for Corfe Castle in 1828. He did stand for East Norfolk in 1832 but was defeated. He died in 1835 and is buried at St Peter's. Apart from impressive memorials to the Peach family in the church it is, at first, not obvious that Nathaniel Peach's short time at Ketteringham had any significant influence on Ketteringham's history. This, however, is not the case as Nathaniel continued with Edward Atkyn's desire to make Ketteringham Park private.

In March 1827 a notice of two highway changes in Ketteringham was published. One was the closure of the highway that leads to Ketteringham Hall from Wymondham (Church Road) which passed north of the Hall joining The Street east of Ivy House Farm. This route could still be used for "any ecclesiastical purposes whatsoever"[20] with the right of free passage to visit church and church yard. Other travellers were required to travel north and join the west end of The Street. To reduce the additional length of this new route a new road was introduced which cut the corner at this junction (see p.70). With Ketteringham Street's new route the former part of The Street was likely given a new name, perhaps due to its slightly lower location or reduced status it became Low Road or Low Street. Following a discussion amongst the village at the end of the 20th century this became standardised as Low Street and what was once called The Street, Ketteringham is now Ketteringham High Street. Although restrictions on the use of the old Highway were made, most of the villagers would have walked to church. A footpath still exists from Ketteringham School to the church. It is odd that no mention is made of this route to the church in the highways closure order. For most, the footpath is the shortest route to the church. This was shown on the sales particulars issued by William Peach only 10 years later in 1837 and it can be assumed that this path had been in existence for some time.

Ketteringham Hall Park was now out-of-bounds to all but invited guests. The church's historic location next to the lord of the manor's residence had, in earlier times, been desirable and advantageous for those who owned Ketteringham Hall. While it still gave the lord the illusion of power and prestige, its proximity to the Hall prevented complete exclusion from the Park. He could not stop those in the parish who wished attending church.

There is some evidence of investment in Ketteringham under Nathaniel Peach. A new blacksmith's house was built in 1831. St Peter's church, however, suggests the parish was rundown. The vicar Rev. Miles Beevor was also rector, at Hethel and Bircham Newton with Tofts. He lived at Mulbarton Hall and only came to Ketteringham as a matter of duty when required. His lack of enthusiasm was replicated by the parishioners who rarely attended his services. Owen Chadwick paints a picture of the church, at the time of Charlotte Atkyns' death, as a building suffering from neglect; even the east window with its fine stained glass had been broken and randomly repaired. He suggests that between 1814 and 1835 the tomb of Sir Henry Grey disappeared from the chancel.

Nathaniel Peach died in 1835 leaving the Ketteringham Estate to his only son William Nathaniel Peach who would put it up for auction in 1837. The appointed auctioneers were Farebrother & Co, 9 Lancaster Place, Strand, London. They produced a catalogue for the sale with much useful information on the estate which included a map of the entire estate.

Being produced at a time when ploughs were drawn by horses and enclosures were small and largely followed the medieval landscape it has proved to be a valuable source of reference for the chapters so far. It has given an insight into how the manor had developed, and what it had become.

The sales description was, "The Ketteringham Estate. Capital Freehold Estate, including nearly the Entire Parish, Mansion, Park, Farms and Woods, lying within a ring fence..". On the front page the auctioneers felt that it would be relevant to mention the estate was lying within a ring fence. Historians divide 19th century parishes into two categories, 'open' and 'closed' parishes. Open parishes had many landowners, a growing population and a diverse economy, whereas closed ones were owned by one or just a few landowners and did not welcome newcomers. The Ketteringham Estate was a closed parish with a single landowner and surrounded by a ring fence. The Atkyn's desire for privacy was seen in their efforts to prevent the villagers from using routes across the grounds of the Hall. It appears they also chose to deter outsiders by a fence around the estate. The mention of this on the front page of the sale document suggests that the auctioneers considered such a fence would make the estate more desirable to a particular purchaser. For some, creating a closed village around their country seat meant they could create a setting of their choosing, one that could impress without the presence of a large and rowdy population and an alehouse. There was another reason that closed parishes had advantages over open ones. The landowner of the parish was responsible for poor relief for those in the parish. A larger population would have had proportionately more sick and needy people, so an 'open' village was less desirable. In 1834, in an attempt to control the cost of poor relief, the Poor Law Amendment Act had been passed by Parliament. This introduced the workhouse as a means of offering relief for the poor. Parishes were formed into unions with each having a workhouse. Ketteringham was in the Poor Law Union of Henstead with its workhouse at Swainsthorpe.[21] The sale particulars bring to the attention of the purchaser that, "the Poor's Rates are extremely small".

The names of Ketteringham's lords and their families are not hard to find but the names of those who inhabited the small dwellings and worked the land are more elusive and often impossible. Since 1695, parish registers have been kept at St Peter's in which the names of those baptised, married and buried in the parish

Norfolk, Five Miles from Norwich.

THE KETTERINGHAM ESTATE.

CAPITAL FREEHOLD ESTATE,

Including nearly the Entire Parish, Mansion, Park, Farms and Woods, lying within a Ring Fence,

AND CONTAINING

TWO THOUSAND ACRES,

WITH THE ADVOWSON OF THE PARISH.

Also, the Manors of Hethersett & Barford Hall, & au Eligible Estate at Barford.

The Particulars and Conditions of Sale

OF THE

DISTINGUISHED AND HIGHLY VALUABLE

FREEHOLD ESTATE,

IN THE VERY BEST PART OF THE

COUNTY OF NORFOLK,

Being about FIVE MILES from NORWICH; consisting of nearly the

ENTIRE PARISH of KETTERINGHAM,

WITH A CAPITAL MANSION,

(OF MODERATE SIZE)

Seated in a BEAUTIFUL PARK, ornamented by a fine Sheet of Water, and pleasingly Wooded and Planted; GARDENS; suitable Offices of every description; and

Several well-arranged FARMS of Meadow, Pasture & Arable Lands,

With convenient FARMING BUILDINGS and COTTAGES for LABOURERS;

EXTENSIVE WOODS, forming FINE PRESERVES FOR GAME.

The Whole Property lying within a RING FENCE, and containing nearly

TWO THOUSAND ACRES,

GREAT TYTHE-FREE.

ALSO, THE

ADVOWSON of KETTERINGHAM.

THE MANSION, (Furnished) and Twenty-eight Acres of Land, with the Right of Sporting, is let until Lady-day next to ALEXANDER OGILBY, Esq.; and the Farms are in the Occupation of highly respectable Tenants, chiefly on Lease.

ALSO,

THE MANOR OF HETHERSETT,

With FINES, QUIT-RENTS, &c.; and the

Manor of Barford Hall and Soame Hall,

With FINES and QUIT RENTS; and

A COMPACT FARM OF PASTURE AND ARABLE LAND,

Let to Mr. JOHN ANGUS, on Lease.

Which will be Sold by Auction,

BY MESSRS.

FAREBROTHER & CO.

At Garraway's Coffee House, 'Change Alley, Cornhill, London.

On **TUESDAY, 30th of MAY, 1837,** at 12 o'Clock,

In Lots, by direction of the Executors, unless an acceptable Offer is previously made by Private Contract.

Descriptive Particulars, with Plans, may be had (and the Estate Viewed by leave of the Tenants One Month prior to the Sale) of Mr. ROBERT WRIGHT, Land Surveyor, Norwich; at the King's Arms, Wymondham; the Angel, Bury St. Edmunds; Greyhound, Newmarket; Cock, Attleburgh; of Mr. ANGUS the Tenant at Barford; of Messrs. KINDERLEY, DENTON and KINDERLEY, Solicitors, Lincoln's Inn New Square; at Garraway's; and at Messrs. FAREBROTHER and CO.'s Offices, 9, Lancaster Place, Strand, London.

Catalogue of sale, 1837.

are recorded. In the churchyard it was becoming the practice for the wealthier to place a gravestone as a memorial to a family member, a practice similar, although more modest, to the memorials to those of the lord in the church. As we come to the end of the Atkyns' time at the Hall, the sale particulars give the name of those who occupied the farms, along with farm details and rent. The potential purchaser was also informed as to the respectability of the tenants.

The information offered by Hunter on the thirty years from 1801 are less personal, but of interest. The number of houses remained at twenty-eight although the population grew from 181 to 215. His analysis of employment in the parish in 1831 shows three employed in retail, nine females, 'without any males' are recorded as servants, while the remainder are all employed in agriculture.[22]

The right to appoint the vicar had played a significant role in Ketteringham's history. It provided the owners of Ketteringham Hall, if not control, a level of influence over St Peter's that might be to their advantage. The sale document states, "With the Advowson of the Parish". Appearing on the first page in bold lettering implies this was considered a desirable feature of the estate. At the time of the sale Ketteringham Hall was in the tenancy of Alexander Ogilby. As tenants the right to present the vicar did not therefore lay with those who lived at the Hall but the owner. The year before Charlotte died, Miles Beevor, the last vicar presented by Edward Atkyns died. Joseph Sewell presented the new vicar William Wayte Andrew in 1835. The Rev. Beevor does not appear to have been a man dedicated to the parish of Ketteringham. The parishioners must have hoped the new vicar would be more committed and work with the purchaser to revive the tired Estate.

Notes

1. Hunter, *The History and Topography of Ketteringham in the county of Norfolk*, p.62.
2. Carter, *The Beevor Story*, p.34.
3. Ibid., p.38.
4. NRO CSCE Book, p.276-7.
5. Ibid.
6. Chadwick, *Victorian Miniature*, p.35.
7. Wade-Martins ed., *An Historic Atlas of Norfolk*, p.124.
8. Sharpe, *Early Modern England: A social history 1550-1760*, p. 136.
9. NRO BOI161.
10. NRO DN/GLE 13/95Kett.
11. The British Newspaper Archive.
12. Ibid.
13. Historic England listing 1306192.
14. Rose, 9515 Ketteringham.
15. Ibid. 10.
16. Jones, *Norwich, Radicalism and the French Revolution:1789-1795*.
17. Wikipedia, Louis XVII.
18. Ibid. 10.
19. Ibid. 1, p.70.
20. NRO CSCE 2/12/4 1827.
21. Ibid. 7, p.142.
22. Ibid. 1, p.62.

The Boileaus

Today, while visiting London, one might pop into a coffee shop to buy a coffee and a piece of cake. In May 1837 John Boileau, or more likely his agent, went into a London coffee house and bought a coffee and a country estate.

In the 19th century, London's Royal Exchange refused to allow stockbrokers entry due to their bad behaviour, so they carried out their dealings at local venues. In the old City of London, between the Royal Exchange in Cornhill and the Post Office in Lombard Street, runs a small alleyway known as Exchange Alley. The coffee shops situated in this alley became ideal meeting places for the trading of shares and commodities. One was called Garraway's where commodities and shares could be auctioned. Here on 30

Garraway's Coffee House in a sketch drawn shortly before demolition in 1866.

May 1837 an auction was held with the first lot being the Ketteringham Estate. The successful bidder on this Lot was John Peter Boileau.

The Boileaus had fled from France due to religious persecution following the French king, Louis XIV, signing the Revocation of the Edict of Nantes in 1685, the year of Lady Mary Heveningham's death. Sir William Heveningham's involvement in the death of a king had resulting in his imprisonment in 1660 which nearly lost him Ketteringham Hall. Charlotte Atkyns' attempt to save a Queen and a future king had lost her Ketteringham Hall. One hundred and thirty years after Charles Boileau was given the right to call himself an Englishman, his great-grandson bought the Ketteringham Estate. He paid £80,000 for the Estate. William Nathaniel Peach received less than £35,000[1] after creditors were satisfied—a clear indication of the financial problems Charlotte Atkyns had created for the Estate.

John Peter Boileau's father (also John Peter) made his fortune in India which, when he returned to England in 1785, he used to purchase Tacolneston Hall about 7.5 km from Ketteringham Hall. His son, before he bought the Ketteringham Estate, had been a magistrate in Fakenham in Norfolk, renting Thursford Hall. On leaving Oxford University he had joined the Rifle Brigade seeing service in the Napoleonic War; only just missing out on being present at the battle of Waterloo. Ketteringham Hall had gone from the hands of the old established family of Heveningham, to a professional lawyer, to a merchant and now to a family who had an aristocratic history, with wealth derived from the British Empire. The connection with the Empire was added to when John married Lady Catherine Sarah Elliot, the 3rd daughter of the Earl of Minto, formerly Governor-General of India. That the Empire was becoming a significant part of both British political and economic life was now reflected in the Ketteringham Estate.[2]

Ketteringham Hall, or The Mansion as it was described in the sale details, was rented out to Alexander Ogilby until Lady-day (26 March) the following year. John Boileau honoured this tenancy agreement possibly because he or the Hall was not ready for him to occupy. No doubt the rental income of £700, which was on par with that from the largest farm on the Estate, did not go amiss.[3] The Ogilbys were pleased to remain for a little longer as they were content living there. It was said that when he finally left the Hall "a rumour reached the parish that he had gone mad and died, crying".[4] It was not until the end of 1838 that the Boileaus moved into Ketteringham Hall. Between purchase and moving in Princess Victoria became Queen. At her coronation she made the new squire of Ketteringham a baronet, a hereditary title above the knighthood but below the peerage. The baronetcy is for Tacolneston[5] not Ketteringham.

Sir John found St Peter's church had an established vicar, the Rev. William Wayte Andrew, who had strong views on the relationship between the Hall and his church. Certain aspects of this relationship will be touched on in this chapter but to appreciate both sides the reader is referred to Owen Chadwick's book, Victorian Miniature. The power struggle between the Hall and church was not new. Since Ketteringham's earliest days, religion had been used as a means of securing the power of the headman and his family. To maintain that power influence, if not control, of how religious practice was undertaken had benefits for the Lord of the Manor. Such desires would invariably be at odds with the religious representative who had felt in matters of religion he was in charge.

The Rev. Andrew had been unable to find suitable accommodation in the parish of Ketteringham and chose to rent nearby Hethel Hall. Sir John, who was in Europe at the time, decided to purchase Hethel Hall and it became the home of his boy's tutor and governess following their marriage. Very laudable that was, but in so doing it made the vicar homeless. The action of making the tenant homeless contrasts with the purchase of Ketteringham Hall where the Oglibys were allowed to remain for the length of their agreement. This left a lasting resentment and tainted the relationship between the parson's wife and the Squire.

John Boileau had paid £80,000 for an Estate which would provide £2138.14s.0d. in rental income,[6] a return of 2.67%. This was not a great return, but it was not a money-making venture. It was a means of entering the establishment by becoming landed gentry. Like the Atkyns before him, he wanted to give the impression that his new family seat was not in fact 'new' but had a long-established family connection. As with the Atkyns, memorials were placed in the chancel of the church to family members who had died before the Estate had any connections to the new owner's family. Sir John followed this tradition but with extra zeal. On his return from his European travels he decided to have a gallery in the church. The reasoning was to create seating for the school children away from the main congregation but, in doing so, he took the opportunity to display to the world the identity of the donor, with his name and coat of arms painted in large gold letters. That it was so prominent to the congregation leaving the church might be significant. The view from the pulpit might be relevant too.

His wife Catherine had always suffered from poor health and when in 1853 she displayed a serious bout of illness it caused Sir John to consider where she might be laid to rest. He knew that under the chancel in 'his' church was a crypt which he felt was a place befitting his family. Secretly, so not to alarm the

Sir John Peter Boileau 1794—1869
by David Octavius Hill and
Robert Adamson.

faculty he sent his carpenter, Mr Hunter, down into the vault where he found many coffins. He said only one was marked with a name, Heron Esp., 1 April 1702. The crypt was full and unhygienic. Thinking no coffins had been placed in the vault for one hundred and fifty years, he wrote to the Bishop of Norwich to ask if he might apply for leave to remove the coffins in the vault and bury them in the churchyard leaving the vault for his family's use. Although agreeing to the request Bishop Hinda advised Sir John that it should be done quietly. The Rev. Andrew also found it questionable but, as the bishop had agreed to it, also accepted the request advising "the removal should take place after dusk, to avoid curiosity". The deed was carried out by Sir John's head gardener Easton and carpenter Hunter who removed five coffins. Apart from Heron's they also found Lady Mary Heveningham's which was broken and its contents scattered. One of the unforeseen results was at the following service on Sunday, the church was full of the stench of decaying bodies from the disturbed crypt. Another, and far more serious one, was a letter from Mr Pemberton of Bourn Hall, Caxton which opens; "Sir, I learn this morning, with the deepest surprise and indignation, that you have ventured to break open the family vault at Ketteringham and directed that the coffins should be all placed in a hole dug by your direction somewhere in the churchyard".

Mr Pemberton was related by marriage to the Peach family and Atkyns from whom Sir John had brought the Estate. Sir John wrote a letter of explanation and apology to Mr Pemberton, but news of his actions became local knowledge. Ballads were composed in the pub houses of Wymondham. Sir John was nicknamed 'Resurrection Jack'. A veiled article appeared in the *Norfolk Chronicle* and Sir John was later named in the *Examiner*.

The coffins were returned to the vault in a service attended by Mr Pemberton, the Dean of Norwich, Rev. Andrew and Mr Clarke (Sir John's solicitor) representing Sir John who did not attend. The vault was bricked up and paved over as it remains today. Mr Pemberton also noted that Sir John had moved the memorial to Mr Peach in order to provide a more prominent position for a memorial to Sir John's family. Sir John returned the Peach memorial to its original position. Lady Catherine's health improved but whether the family should eventually be laid to rest in a grave or vault remained. Sir John's solution to this

The Boileau Mausoleum, before restoration, 2004.

problem was the erection of a family mausoleum in the churchyard, but not before he had undertaken much research into possible challenges and offence it might cause.[7] The mausoleum[8] was restored in 2006 under the guidance of the current church warden Dr Mary Parker.

Sir John's diaries[9] give an insight as to how he viewed his position as Squire and the corresponding duty he felt to those who dwelt on the Ketteringham Estate. He considered himself to be 'the father of the parish'. He visited the poor. He visited his tenants when they were sick or bereaved. If they could justify not being at work, he still paid their wages reducing the fear of the workhouse. He gave them coal at Christmas and in January, the poor were treated to a roast beef dinner with plum pudding and ale. As father of the parish he also worried about their moral and spiritual well-being. Dissenters were not allowed to be tenants and he expected all to attend church. There was no public house in the village. Sir John records in his diaries how the tenants were invited to feast at the Hall. He held a Christmas dance for his servants. These were opportunities for Sir John to treat those on his Estate as an extended family. Sir John, like Miss Atkyns, expected the boys to be taught. He paid for a new school building and teacher which opened in the village on 28 January 1840. The tenants expected the Squire to look after their interests and it appears that Sir John took this seriously, but, in return, loyalty was expected from them. In a time before mass franchise and the secret ballot, the extent of this loyalty is apparent in comments made in 1845 by an agent in Ketteringham regarding a reference for a prospective tenant on a neighbouring estate. He wrote, "I don't know whether you think of your tenants' politics, but Alden's family have always acted against us here".

The relationship between the Hall and its tenant played an important part in Ketteringham's history. The relationship between neighbouring Stanfield Hall and a tenant would, in 1848, become part of Ketteringham's history. Stanfield Hall had become the home of the lawyer, Isaac Jermy. Isaac Jermy's real name was Preston, but on taking charge of the Stanfield Estate he chose to take the name of the previous owners. Some members of the Jermy family, a Mr Larner in particular, felt the estate should have gone to a "true" Jermy and not Isaac "Preston". The strength of feel regarding this perceived injustice was so strong that in September 1838 Mr Larner, along with eighty others, besieged the Hall. James Rush was bailiff on the Stanfield Hall Estate and the tenant of Potash Farm, about 1.75 km from Ketteringham Hall. He chose to attend St Peter's, Ketteringham. Rush had financial difficulties and had mortgaged and re-mortgaged his farm. This, combined with the knowledge of a possible weakness in the Squire's right to the Stanfield Hall Estate, resulted in him constructing a plan that might get him out of his financial problem. Rush disguised himself and went to Stanfield Hall where he shot dead both Isaac Jermy and his son hoping the rival claimants would be blamed. When the police came, they went to Potash Farm to question Rush. His governess and mistress Emily Sandford acted as his alibi claiming Rush was only out for a few minutes but later retracted her statement and Rush was arrested. The story of the murders and trial in April 1849 became

James Blomfield Rush, portrait of Rush sketched in court.

Death mask of James Rush.

national news. Sir John Boileau was one of the examining magistrates at the trial and, as Rush attended St Peter's, the Rev. Andrew went to offer pastoral care during Rush's confinement at Norwich Castle. Rush was found guilty and hung from the bridge over the moat at Norwich Castle. The interest in the press resulted in between twelve and thirteen thousand people seeing, what would be in Norwich, the last public execution. Such was the national interest that a wax representation of James Rush was displayed in the Chamber of Horrors at Madam Tussauds from 1849 until 1936. It was then donated to The Wellcome Library. Charles Dickens visited Stanfield Hall and wrote of a search being conducted between the Hall and Potash Farm. Even Queen Victoria was known to have been interested in the outcome of the trial.

The national interest and its outcome spilled over to all who had been involved. The Rev. Andrew turned up at St Peter's to give his sermon the following Sunday only to find many people now wanted to see and hear the priest who visited the condemned man. He had to announce his sermon would be postponed until the following Sunday. When he did give the sermon it is estimated that the number in the church and churchyard was two thousand. He preached for two hours twenty minutes. The sermon was printed in the newspaper. Andrew decided, reluctantly, to publish it himself. It sold well at 3d. St Peter's vicar, for short a period at least, became known beyond his small parish of Ketteringham.

The Stanfield murders gave Ketteringham and its vicar a moment in the limelight. Sir John had little interest in the popular press and preferred to associate himself with the 'important' people of the time. He entertained distinguished visitors at Ketteringham Hall and seemed happy that many of their visits were mentioned in the newspapers. In 1848, an article appeared in *The Morning Post* mentioning, His Royal Highness Prince Leopold of Naples (Count Salerno) who had paid a visit to Ketteringham Hall.

Sir John made many improvements to his Estate the most obvious of which can be seen in Ketteringham Hall. The building he bought was basically the Elizabethan Hall dating largely from the time of the Heveninghams. It had been damaged by fire in 1806 and needed repair and improvement. In 1840 he had a Gothic Hall built on the side of the building. This was so he could entertain with balls and banquets. It was also the venue where the Squire gave feasts in a medieval setting in keeping with 'merry old England' which, thanks to people like Sir Walter Scott, were popular and would likely have appealed to Sir John's antiquarian interests, when not in use it was where the servants ate. He employed the service of Thomas Allason, who at the same time constructed an orangery. In 1852 he employed another architect, Thomas Jeckell who enlarged the Tudor Hall by infilling and added Gothic features. These included a Gothic doorway with shields displaying John Peter Boileau and Catherine Boileau' initials. Gothic architecture was the fashion of the period. When the prime minister, Disraeli, brought his country house he spent a large amount of money recreating what he believed a medieval house would have looked like. Sir John wanted to do likewise but with smaller funds. Jeckell was also employed to design wrought iron work for a rose pergola in the garden and projects around Ketteringham village such as designing the well at Wellgate Cottages.

Norwich is by far the most important settlement in the vicinity and Norwich Lodge, one of the Park's five lodges, would be expected to be the grandest. Jeckell was employed to design a suitable lodge with a gate keeper. Jeckell specified the wood to be used for the gate suggesting this entrance was intended to make an impression to those visiting the Hall. The lodge was built in 1849.

The lodge is situated on a hill. Passing through its gate the visitor could appreciate

Ketteringham Hall in the second half of the 19th century.

the open parkland as their carriage drove down to the newly enhanced Hall. The course of driveway provided views of one of the lakes. On the far side Sir John had an icehouse built in 1842. Built in a similar style to the Hall it not only gave a supply of ice at a time before refrigeration but enhanced the Hall's setting.

The arrival at the Hall from Wymondham was also made grander. The enclosure road that crossed the old common was turned into an oak lined avenue leading up to Wymondham Lodge. Here a new avenue of oaks continued straight before passing through a dark yew wood then sweeping into the light in front of the Hall. The new avenue from the lodge was planted to commemorate Sir John's appointment as High Sheriff of Norfolk in1844 hence the name Sheriff's Avenue.

Sir John intended to regain the prestige of the Estate lost in the time of Charlotte Atkyns. Just as Charlotte had taken in those fleeing the uprising in France so Sir John gave temporary refuge to François Guizot, the French Prime Minister. He had resigned over the unrest in Paris, unrest which led to the second French Republic. Ketteringham Hall saw many other distinguished visitors including Bishop Stanley (Norwich), Lord Braybrook, the historian Hallam and from Norwich, Amelia Opie.

The icehouse, 2015.

Sir John showed an interested in science and literature. He was vice-president of many societies and institutes including the Zoological Society, the

Burgh Castle, bought by Sir John Boileau in 1849, 2020.

Royal Statistical Society, the Institute of Archaeology, the Royal Society of Arts, the Society of Antiquaries of London, the Royal Institution and the British Science Association. In 1843 he was elected as a Fellow of the Royal Society and was a Fellow of the Geological Society of London. It is not clear how actively he was involved in all of these. His interest in antiquities was perhaps the most important to him and he played a major role in the Norfolk Archaeological Society becoming their president in 1849. He excavated one of the burial mounds at Five Ways. He purchased Burgh Castle,[10] a Roman site on the Great Estuary near Great Yarmouth, to preserve the ruins and encouraged excavation work there.

Although those like Sir John, as gentlemen, may have had the time to pursue intellectual endeavours, the people of Ketteringham did not. Owen Chadwick records that Lady Catherine, while walking in the village, met Mrs Durrant who expressed her concerns about the story circulating in Ketteringham and Hethersett that Queen Victoria had ordered all children under five to be killed. It turned out, on investigation into this pending crime, that the Poor Law authorities had ordered that all children in the poor house be vaccinated.

Like his father, Sir John's youngest son, Charles Boileau joined the British Army. As a member of the Rifles in the Crimean War he advanced on the Redan at Sebastopol. He was shot in the leg but continued the advance and was shot again, the bullet just missed his heart and lodged in his hip. On his way back to England he died in a temporary hospital in Malta. A monument to Charles was placed on the north wall of the chancel. Charles Boileau was the first in Ketteringham to die, not in defence of his home or his country, but for the British Empire. Ketteringham in the past had, in matters of war, felt the impact of decisions made by groups overseas. Britain had become a world power. Ketteringham, like other communities, would be affected by decisions made in London on matters of Empire.

On 5 November 1836 an announcement appeared in the *Norfolk Chronicle* stating that a footpath running from High Ash to Smeeth, Ketteringham would be replaced on 4 January 1837. That the announcement, despite being on private land, had to be published in a newspaper suggests that the Squire was not totally free to do as he wished. Whether this showed a loss of power is arguable as it is uncertain if any member of the village challenged his wish. The notification refers to the length of both the existing and the new route. Today a footpath in the countryside might be considered a pleasant walk. Most footpaths, however, originated as the shortest route between two locations when the primary method of travel was on foot and time was of the essence.

Eight years later the importance of human physical effort would be recorded in a newspaper report of the new railway that was under construction between Norwich and Brandon: "More than 1000 men on the Brandon line with a great many at Ketteringham. 3000 before Christmas being paid 2s 9d a day. The consumption of so many labourers must cause a good deal of money to be circulated in the villages for food alone, for although the men are supplied by the 'Tommy Shops' these must first obtain a stock of provisions from nearby markets".[11] The article gives an indication of the manpower required to build a railway at a time before mechanisation and the problems a sudden influx of migrant workers would pose. Sir John received payment for the loss of land and stipulated that any temporary land used for spoil must only be used for that purpose and be immediately returned at the end of construction. Despite the amount of work involved to dig the cutting by hand and the sad loss of a man's life a year later, the paper recorded the opening of the Norfolk Railway on 26 July 1845. The article referred to the climb to Ketteringham Woods as 35ft per mile then the decline as 2ft per mile this being the highest point on the line.[12]

At a time when the length of a footpath was considered important, it is not hard to imagine the monumental change brought about by the ability to travel greater distances by train. This is highlighted by that fact it was previously quicker to go from Norwich to Amsterdam by sea than to London by road. This comparison is for passenger travel and although freight was carried on the new railways much still travelled by water. The Great Estuary that drains into the North Sea also experienced improvements with canals being

The New Cut, Haddiscoe, 2010.

The Easterling locomotive going under the bridge built to allow livestock from Station Farm to access pasture in Ketteringham, 2013.

constructed and water ways being made navigable. Ketteringham's access to this water system since Anglo-Saxon times had been through Norwich. Norwich's links with the North Sea were improved by the construction of New Cut in 1833 which went from Reedham to Haddiscoe linking the River Yare and Waveney to the new harbour of Lowestoft with cheaper port tolls than those of Great Yarmouth.

Sir John insisted that certain features be incorporated into the new railway line that crossed his land. A bridge was built on Wash Lane (now Ketteringham Lane). A bridge was also built to allow livestock to cross from his Hethersett dairy farm (later known as Station Farm) to its pasture over the railway in Ketteringham. Although useful for people on foot its main purpose was to allow the safe passage for cattle and other livestock over the track. A station was built at Hethersett just beyond the boundary with Ketteringham. An additional small station was built at Spinks Lane just beyond Ketteringham's western boundary. It is assumed it was little used as it only remained in operation for five months.[13] Sir John insisted that one train in each direction stop at Hethersett Station every day.

The grand new drive from Wymondham must have pleased him as he often used the new Wymondham station when going to or returning from London. (The new line to Brandon connected with the line to Shoreditch.) It would likely have impressed his many visitors too. Sir John and his family went to London every year for the Season. This required two first-class carriages for his family, two second-class carriages for the servants, a truck and a horsebox. Such an endeavour would have been very trying by road.

With the construction of railway lines, cables for telegraph system were laid alongside the track. In 1853 this allowed Sir John to receive a telegram in London informing him that his wife Catherine was ill. On finding the last train to Wymondham had gone he was given a price of £45 to hire a special train, he waited for the morning train. The railway gave the village boys in Ketteringham a new challenge, hitting the train with a stone as it passed under the bridge at Wash Lane. The blacksmith's son, Walter Thrower was convicted of throwing stones which hit the engine's stoker.

Ketteringham villagers had been using Wymondham market since it gained its charter in 1139. The railway was of mixed blessings for Ketteringham's old neighbour. From 1851 its population began to decline. In 1881 its market was described as "almost extinct owing to the great facilities provided by the railway for attending Norwich market".[14] The ability to use the larger Norwich market rather than the "almost extinct" market at Wymondham was an option open for villagers in Ketteringham. The railway allowed the transportation of materials across country. Welsh slate became common for roofs such as Ketteringham's new schoolhouse.

In 1854, Ketteringham had a harvest estimated to be 20% more than usual and Sir John suggested to the Rev. Andrew that, following the harvest festival, they should hold a dinner in the grounds for the poor of the village. This was during the period of Victorian high farming when fertilizers such as bonemeal and guano imported from South America improved crop yield. New animal breeds were developed. Sir John was keen on agricultural improvement although he tended to suggest others, his tenants, should implement them. He employed a London-based Civil Engineer, Hamilton Fulton, to investigate improving drainage at Hethel Wood Farm. (Hethel Wood Farm was purchased by Sir John in 1850 and renamed as such as it was the Potash Farm of the murderer James Rush.) The location of Ketteringham on the edge of the heavy clay had meant that much drainage work had taken place for hundreds of years. A system of drainage ditches exists which, on the west side of the village channels water to the river Tiffey, on the south side to Ketteringham Hall Lake and the north side to Hethersett Hall Lake. All ultimately feeding into the Yare then the Wensum valley. A culvert was constructed to run under Sir John's Sheriff's Avenue, suggesting that he may have had at least some of the village's drainage system improved when work was carried out on the Hall's new entrance way.

It was around this time that the farm buildings associated with Hall Farm (Home Farm) were replaced by new, more efficient, farm buildings to the west of the farmhouse (the former rectoral property appropriated to the Prior of Pentney).

In 1898, the pair of cottages north of High Ash Road were knocked down leaving some small barns. This was part of an ongoing process of improvements to Ketteringham's farms. Modern farming is often blamed for grubbing up hedges, but a comparison between the sales map of 1837 and the smaller part of the parish covered by the first OS of 1882 shows that 3.3 km of hedgerow had been removed. Many of the irregular boundaries, a relic of the carving out of closes from the open field system, were removed to create larger enclosures. A survey of the Estate was carried out for Sir John. It recorded two acreages against the enclosure names indicating that enclosure enlargement happened soon after he bought the Estate. The medieval farming landscape of Ketteringham was being replaced by a modern one.

In 1868 Sir John, suffering from bad health moved to Torquay and died in the spring the following year. He had bought the bankrupted Ketteringham Estate and turned it into a modern Victorian Estate of which he was proud. He had seen the 'Golden Years' of the English Estate as it flourished on the back of growing agricultural wealth, shared the pride in Empire and enjoyed the benefits of the industrial revolution.

On his death in 1869 his son, Francis, inherited the Ketteringham Estate. He became Baronet of Tacolneston and the census of 1871 records Sir Francis as residing at Tacolneston Hall his manorial home. The census ten years later shows he had moved to Ketteringham Hall. Tacolneston Hall was let to a Member of Parliament, George Edward Price. It is possible the decision to move to Ketteringham Hall was personal preference but more likely the move was for financial reasons with the running of two mansions becoming a burden. If so, he was not alone; 1880 is considered by many historians as a turning point in the fortunes of the country estates.

The railway was the first of the great technological advancements of the industrial age to have an impact on Ketteringham. The railways made it possible to transport large quantities of goods at greater speed than before. Steam engines not only power locomotives, but they also replaced wind as a means of propulsion for ships. Sir John records in his journal in 1846, just four years after the construction of his new ice house, "Wenham ice (clear, clean ice imported from North America) which is 10s /cwt and which they send by railway and charge nothing for packaging, returns".[15] In the decade after Sir John's death, the cost of freight between New York and Liverpool fell by a half and the cost of transporting freight from Chicago to New York by the new railroad also fell. The export of wheat from the USA doubled, Russian exports increased and Canada began exporting. The year of Sir John's death saw the opening of the Suez Canal which resulted in India exporting wheat to Europe and, within ten years, Australia would also be exporting. With cheap transport and the opening of virgin lands for agriculture, the price of grain fell. This, combined with the repeal of the Corn Law in 1846, had profound effects on the economics of cereal growers in Britain.

Initially only cereal growers experienced the impact of cheap grain imports. But another new technology added to the agricultural woes, the development of refrigeration. The USA started exporting chilled, then frozen meat to Europe in 1879. Australia began exporting to Europe the following year. This combined to produce an agricultural depression and coincided with a world economic recession. At the time this was called the 'Great Depression' but to distinguish it from the 'Great Depression' of the 1930s it is now commonly called the 'Long Depression'. There had been several bad summers in Britain in the late 1870s which, at first, was perceived to be the problem. Many of the Norfolk estates experienced rent arrears and agreed to late payments expecting things would improve. It gradually became apparent to the landowners that it was becoming less likely the mounting debts would be repaid. Realising that the problem was more serious than a few bad harvests, from 1885 the landowners cut rents. An example of the decline in rental income in Norfolk can be seen at Boyland Hall near Long Stratton where rents declined from £3,673 in 1877 to £2,224, ten years later in 1896 they had fallen to £1,611.[16]

The Ketteringham Estate as situated in the parish of Ketteringham was only 1,606 acres but, by 1883, the Norfolk landholding of the Boileaus was 3,626 acres. This made Sir Francis Boileau a member of the greater gentry of Norfolk.[17] The census of 1881 records the population of Ketteringham as 210. In 1853 Francis White's Gazetteer records that, apart from those employed at the Hall, Ketteringham's economy was agriculture.[18] The effect of the Long Depression on the rental income of the Ketteringham Estate is not known but, with a large landholding, it is probable that rents were reduced with a corresponding negative impact on the Estate's income.

When Sir Francis inherited the Estate he became patron of St Peter's. He commissioned Thomas Jeckell to raise and adorn the church tower and added a clock to fulfil his father's will. He made some improvements to the Hall, although not on the same grand scale as his father. When approaching the park from Wymondham, rather than using the drive along Sheriff's Avenue followed by the sweeping curve to the front on the Hall, he favoured the more direct route of Church Road. Although a more modest entrance he did mark the entrance to the Park with large stone gate-piers with his wife's initials LHB Lucy Henrietta Boileau on right gate-pier[19] and his, FGMB on the

The entrance from Church Road with its pinnacles, 2004.

left.[20] On top of each pillar, he installed pinnacles originally intended for the Hall. Before the entrance, at the side road to the church, he erected a stone finger guidepost indicating the Hall was to the left and church to the right. In 1899 he continued his father's Gothic theme with gate turrets and projecting parapets on a new stable yard. He shared his father's interest in antiquities and was also a Fellow of the Society of Antiquaries. Into the brickwork of the towers of the yard he placed Greek stela relief marble dating from the second century BCE.[21] In 1878 he bought the medieval masonry from the west window of Norwich Cathedral and erected it by the lake as a folly, called 'the Abbey'. He added other features to the garden, such as the loft gazebo[22] built in the walled kitchen garden in 1898. A

The Greek stela relief, 2004.

new Sunday school was built next to the old vicarage, opened 3 December 1898. Here not only were the children taught the Christian story but the vicar, Rev. T.C. Des Barres, used it as a venue to present lectures. These improvements suggest that the Ketteringham Estate, or this branch of the Boileau family, was not having the same financial problems as other Norfolk estates. The Boileau were fortunate in having an additional income from property in London, cushioning the Estate from the economic hardship experienced by other Norfolk estates.

Sir Francis died in 1900 and chose not to be laid to rest with his parents in the mausoleum his father had built for the family but in a grave next to it. He may not have wanted to be associated with the upset behind the construction of the building. At the start of the end of the 19th century, aristocratic displays of grandeur were less in favour and a simple grave may have been more to his liking. Possibly this was the reason he chose to abandon the grand drive from Wymondham in favour of the functional route to the Hall still in use today. Society was changing but the historic event at the start of this book still hung over the Estate. To build the new stables a walnut tree had to be cut down. This was the tree planted by Lady Mary Heveningham in 1660 to commemorate the restoration. Despite it being 339 years since Sir William Heveningham had been found guilty of treason, Sir Francis still felt he should mark the spot where the tree once stood with a plaque in the wall.

Three years before his death in June 1897 he erected a monument at Five Ways to commemorate the 60th year of Queen Victoria's reign.[23]

'The Abbey' folly, 2004.

The ownership of the Ketteringham Estate had, with the Boileaus, returned to a family with an aristocratic past. Although it was a lost French aristocracy, the Heveninghams might have been gratified to see their Estate in such hands. The rise of many professionals such as lawyers, which had alarmed Sir Arthur Heveningham so much, bought estates in the 17th century and 18th century. The landed gentry had accommodated the rise of new groups joining its ranks. In the 19th century, the professionals were joined by another group keen to purchase estates. These men had made money from trade and the opportunities the Empire offered and once wealthy could buy an estate and join the landed gentry. The Boileaus had done just that and regained the prestige of their lost French aristocratic background by becoming members of Norfolk's greater gentry. The new technology of the railways ran through Estate lands but the Ketteringham Estate, like most Norfolk estates, remained an agricultural economy not dissimilar to what it had been from earlier times. With such a limited economic base, the estates were not in a strong position.

The growth of manufacturing and commerce meant that by the 1880s the power base shifted. The new industries were creating large profits while agriculture was not. The population of England and Wales rose between 1781 and 1881 from 7.5 million to 26 million.[24] The population growth meant that the country was unable to produce sufficient food and became reliant on imported food. British trade was now based largely on manufacturing and commerce with its success in world markets more than covering the cost of food imports. This resulted in a growing importance for manufacturing and commerce and a corresponding reduction in that of agriculture. The change in importance of these two groups is reflected in the country's power base. By 1885 the landed class no longer had a clear majority in the House of Commons and, twenty-five years later, lost their overriding influence in the House of Lords.

The Boileaus had survived the economic hard times and were even able to invest in both Ketteringham Hall and the Estate. The Hall that exists today is as a result of their investments. When Sir Francis died, they were not forced to sell to the new manufacturing or financial class and the Estate passed to his son Maurice.

Notes

1. *History of Parliament Vol. 1820-1832*, entry for William Nathaniel Peach.
2. Chadwick, *Victorian Miniature*, p.58-9.
3. Farebrother & Co, Sales Catalogue, p.4.
4. Ibid. 2, p.38.
5. The baronetcy refers to Tacolestone the village is Tacoleston.
6. Ibid. 3, p.11.
7. Ibid. 2, p.132-46.
8. Historic England listing IOE01/16047/16.
9. Ref to Sir John's Journal NRO.
10. NHER 10471.
11. The British Newspaper Archive.
12. Ibid.
13. Miller, *Early Railway happenings in South Norfolk*, p.6.
14. Wade-Martins, *Norwich a changing countryside*, p.88.
15. NRO Boi 69117x4 p363.
16. Barnes, *Norfolk Landowners since 1880*, p.17.
17. Ibid., p.85.
18. *White's, History, Gazetteer, and Directory of Norfolk 1854*, p.513.
19. Ibid. 8, listing 1170070.
20. Ibid. 1050551.
21. Ibid. 1170116.
22. Ibid. 1306192.
23. Ibid. 1050554.
24. Ibid. 16, p.11.

The Great War & Second World War

Maurice came to inherited Ketteringham on the cusp of a new era. The following year Queen Victoria died and the Edwardian age began. Sir Maurice planted an oak tree in the Park to commemorate the occasion. The 1901 national census records Ketteringham as having 41 houses and four uninhabited houses (of which one is confusingly recorded as being habited suggesting unofficial habitation). The population was 185 of which 86 were men and 99 were women[1]. Like his grandfather, Sir Maurice kept a journal.[2] Although not as personal as Sir John's it shows he too felt a paternal duty to the Estate, painstakingly recording the births, deaths and marriages of those on the Estate.

His entry for July 1901 records: David Groom, working on Walker's Farm, joined the Norfolk Regiment and started for South Africa. In March 1902 Charles Walker of Ivy House Farm went to take some horses to South Africa. He returned after a little while.

David Groom had gone to fight in the Boer War. He, like Francis' nephew Charles Boileau, had gone to fight on behalf of the Empire not in defence of his country. Ketteringham's Ivy House farm was supplying horses to the Empire. The Empire was playing a part in the lives of the ordinary folks of Ketteringham. On 24 May 1902, on what would have been the Queen's birthday, 'Empire Day' was introduced. Its purpose to remind children that they were part of the British Empire in common with other children across the world and the strength of the Empire depended on them. At schools across the world children sang patriotic songs to Britain, the motherland, a sound likely heard in the school room at Ketteringham. The Empire's purpose was to 'civilise' the world and all should want to serve in this. The importance of service to help others was not lost on Sir Maurice. He had affection for children, not only of the village but a concern for those living further afield in London. In his journal he records:

23 July 1908—Ten Hackney children come to the village for a fortnight. They are taken into the cottages of Mrs. Wade, the two Mrs. Goodrums, Mrs. Allen, and Mrs. John Tooke.

6th to 20th August 1908—Some more London children, 9 in number, come to the village, and are taken in at various cottages as on the former occasion. These came to our annual school treat on the 10th, and the former party spent an afternoon in our grounds on the 4th.

Sir John had brought the technology of the 19th century to Ketteringham with the railways. His grandsons would bring 20th technology to the village. Sir Maurice writes that, in 1905 his brother "Raymond went into Norwich to fetch a Darracq motor which he had bought". In 1911, Sir Maurice took delivery of a Napier and employed Harry Gardener as his chauffeur. Sir Maurice had electric lights installed for the new tenants, Major Denny and his family at Tacolneston Hall.

Vintage cars in Ketteringham, 2008.

Ketteringham even had its own post office. In 1908 the Ketteringham Rovers Football team was formed and played in Ketteringham Hall grounds. The Ketteringham cricket club had been in existence since 1901, although apart from an all-day match on August bank holiday 1906 (against Nelson which Ketteringham won) there are no mentions in his journal of any further matches played in either sport against visiting teams. Life in Ketteringham had moved into the 20th century and life from these extracts from the Squire's journal suggest it was not unpleasant. An article was published in 1906 even describing Ketteringham as a paradise, although that was in reference to teetotallers as it praised the village for not having a pub. However, Sir Maurice's journal also shows that some of the fears of the 19th century still haunted the early 20th century villagers. In June 1904: "Mrs Gray (widow) who had been living in one of my Carlton cottages left the parish today to go to the workhouse". The following month Sir Maurice writes that a former tenant of his father, William Catchpole, died in the workhouse.

Ketteringham people, like other communities in England, had always feared disease coming into their village. In November 1910, Bessie Betts came from Norwich to visit her parents at Folgate Cottage and, in so doing, brought diphtheria to the family. The eldest son John came home on leave but was unable to enjoy his family as they were in quarantine. Despite the cottage being disinfected, the disease returned ten months later. This time it spread to the school which, like the Sunday school, was closed for three weeks. The Betts's seven-year-old son Thomas died.

In the spring of 1912, the 16th Lancers competed in Point-to-Point races in Hethersett but their programme was disrupted by a telegram instructing the regiment to proceed to Wigan where a coal strike was in progress. This was a national coal strike in support of a minimum wage for miners. As a result of the strike the government passed the Coal Mines (Minimum Wage) Act.

When Sir Maurice inherited the Ketteringham Estate he also took responsibility for the medieval Church of St Peter's. Like his father, and a long line of patrons before him, he found it in need of constant maintenance and repair. In 1907 a monument was placed in the church to Charlotte Atkyns. The Frederic Barbey's book, *A Friend of Marie-Antoinette*, had been published two years earlier which might have been the reason that Prince Frederick Duleep Singh and the Rev. Edmund Farrer, chose to come by car from Thetford to view the new monument *(see p.77)*. Whether this visit caused the Boileau embarrassment as to the state of repair of the church is not recorded but two months later Lady Boileau requested that the vicar, Canon Still, meet with her in the church to discuss major repairs to the medieval building.[3] That December, after considering three estimates, the contract for restoration was placed with Mr Stith. This was to replace the roof with one of oak and carving, to underpin and strengthen the walls, reopen a lancet in the chancel, take out and rearrange the glass in the east window and install in a new frame, remove the buttresses at the east end and repair the porch. For such a major project Sir Maurice had to pay the sum of £1220. Work started in the spring of 1908 with the removal of the old roof, the timbers of which were suffering from dry rot and were burnt. The pitch of the new roof was different from the original so the north and south walls were raised by 3 feet.

There is, in the Norfolk Record Office, a single page from a magazine with a piece entitled 'Notable Farms'.[4] This records a visit to Ivy House Farm in Ketteringham on the 13 November 1912. It gives a wonderful insight into farming on the Ketteringham Estate in the early part of the 20th century. The farm was then occupied by

Prince Frederick Victor Duleep Singh.

Arthur Walker. He farmed 427 acres which, apart from 60 acres of pasture, was arable. In addition, he rented 80 acres of parkland. Mr Walker had switched from beef cattle to dairy and was building up a herd of Lincoln red shorthorns. The farm grew crops on a four-course system with 60 acres being planted to oats every year. In small areas he planted specific grasses, lucerne and sainfoin, as an alternative to clover. The main crop was wheat with 7-8 acres of potatoes, 12 acres of maize (referred to at the time as Indian corn) for cattle fodder along with mangels and cabbages also for fodder. In 1912 he tried growing a new crop on his land, sugar beet. That year saw the opening of the Cantley factory for the processing of sugar beet. Built by the Dutch, it was the first successful one in Britain. The crop was clearly new to the writer and reader as great detail is given as to how it was grown and harvested along with the sale price, 21s 6d per ton delivered to the sender's station. Hethersett station was conveniently next to the farm's fields. However, Mr Walker is quoted as saying, "I think it very possible that there would have been a better result had the land been devoted to mangels. But it can hardly be a crop that will lose money". He further went on to talk of the potential of the crop for local employment. While explaining the soil requirements, in addition to dung being added to the field he used "artificials". The adding of man-made fertilizers is an important point in the development of farming in Ketteringham and farming in general. In this case it was bone and superphosphate and Kainit (potash). Kainit was manufactured in Germany. Britain was no longer the only industrial nation. The farm had 15 working horses and half a dozen colts, but now used a Petter Oil engine for "chaffing". Having used it for several years he noted how satisfied he was with it.

As well as dairy cattle the farm had 125 ewes, a cross between the Cotswold and the black-faced Suffolk sheep. This was a large farm by Norfolk standards, clearly well run and Mr Walker was embracing modern science and technology. But farming was still a labour-intensive process and labour had to be paid and housed. The standard wage for this part of Norfolk was 13s a week, although the magazine article points out "that does not mean total earnings, as everyone connected with the land will understand".

Arthur Walker explains that there were insufficient houses for his workers, many of whom had to live in neighbouring villages, but the expense of building new ones could not be met by the higher rent he could charge while the men were so lowly paid. Mr Walker clearly saw his farm as a business, He kept detailed records of his new venture in dairy farming recording the milk yields of all his animals. It may have been his economic thinking that gave him his concern for the low wages, but it was more likely strong Methodist beliefs.

The history of Ketteringham is often determined by discussions and actions made far away from its parish boundaries. The action of one man in the summer of 1914 is perhaps the greatest example of this. Gavrilo Princip, assassinated the

Archduke Franz Ferdinand of Austria in the Bosnian capital Sarajevo triggering the Great War, commonly referred to as the First World War.

Britain was a maritime nation. The British Empire was underpinned by the Royal Navy. When Germany disregarded Britain's request to respect Belgian's neutrality, it was Churchill, as chief of the admiralty that flashed the signal to HM Ships and Naval Establishments:

4 August 1914 Admiralty 11pm
COMMENCE HOSTILITIES AGAINST GERMANY.

Norfolk, with its long coastline and many fishing ports has deep connections with the sea and the Navy. The first service men to be called up in the days before the outbreak of the war were the Royal Navy Reserve. On Sunday 2 August, motor cars left Norwich to travel

Archduke Franz Ferdinand whose assassination started the Great War.

to neighbouring villages to inform men of the call up and a cutter went into the Wash to tell the fishing fleet.[5] On 8 August the government passed the Defence of the Realm act which, amongst other things, allowed for the requisition of horses, wagons and transport equipment. On 17 October 1914 Great Yarmouth was shelled by Imperial German battleships. Plans were made in case Norfolk suffered heavy bombardment or was invaded. This would most likely be a seaborne attack and/or invasion with Great Yarmouth being the most vulnerable. Instructions as to the roads that were to be used for the evacuation were given. In 1916 'Secret' orders were sent to GER (Great Eastern Railways) that in the event of an invasion, the people of Norwich should be removed to Wymondham and beyond. It stated that trains should not stop to pick up passengers, so no stopping was allowed at Hethersett station.[6]

Although the initial call was for Navy Reservists, Britain, unlike most other countries, did not have a system of conscription and therefore a call went out for men to volunteer. Those the country needed most were former soldiers like Ketteringham's David Groom who had served in the Norfolk Regiment during the Boer War, John Betts who had left at 18 to join the Norfolk Regiment in South Africa in 1906 and Walter Delph who had left the army in 1906. William Beaumont returned from several years as a soldier in India in 1908. It is probable they re-joined their regiment as the call went out. General Kitchener (also a Boer War veteran) made what was to become his famous plea, 'Your country needs you' as the need for more men became apparent. The response was especially strong in Norfolk, allowing Kitchener to add to the Norfolk Regiment new battalions of the 7th, 8th, 9th and 10th Service Battalion and the 11th Battalion Territorial Force and the Norfolk Yeomanry Battalion. We do not know the exact number who initially joined from Ketteringham, but in January 1916 all single men and widowers between eighteen and forty-one were conscripted then later, in May, all men in this age group. In 1918, all men up to fifty were included with the power to raise it to fifty-six. Men in Ketteringham must have been thin on the ground.

William Beaumont's brother, or cousin, Arthur George Beaumont joined the 9th Norfolk Regiment in Norwich in September 1914. After training, on the 30 August, they arrived in France. Their first taste of military action was an attack on Lonely Tree Hill, west of Hullach on 26 September. Arthur died that day[7]. George Betts joined the Territorial Force 1/4th Battalion mobilized at the Drill Hall on Chapel Field, Norwich. The battalion was sent overseas landing at Suzla Bay, on the 10 August 1915 and served throughout the Gallipoli Campaign. In December 1915 they went to the Middle East, landing in Alexandria, Egypt. Here on 2 November 1917, Mr & Mrs John Betts of Ketteringham lost their son George.[8] It is not clear whether the John Betts, who also died in the Great War, is related. Walter Henry Dawson died in Palestine in April of that year at the second battle of Gaza, the twenty-nine-year-old son of George and Anna Read of Ketteringham.[9] Cecil Humphreys a bricklayer in Ketteringham, became a Lance Corporal in the Royal Engineers and was killed in action in Flanders/France 10 July 1916.[10] Reginald William Tooke of the Norfolk Regiment died in action 27 July 1916, he was only twenty years old.[11] The deaths were a tragedy to their families and a loss felt by all.

In his journal Sir Maurice records John Page leaving the village school and starting work in 1903 with the Squires. He writes in 1907 of the confirmation at Hethersett, "we drove in with Smart, Miss Collings, Rhoda Beaumont and Bessie Emms, two later were Confirmed. Others from village who likewise received the rite were Ernest Groom (age 25), Frank Dermedy, Ernest Dawson and John Page". Sir Maurice had chosen to record John Page's first job and seen him Confirmed at eighteen. He must have shared the sorrow when he too, fell in Flanders. This fatherly attitude towards the village was shown in 1914 when he gave land and built a wooden village hall for the community near the village school. For over a century the hall has been, and still is, an important venue for social events in the village. Sir Maurice's younger brother Raymond had become a Major in the Royal Fusiliers and the Royal Garrison Artillery and became an acting Lieutenant Colonel serving in France where he was mentioned in dispatches.

As the casualties of war mounted, sixty-two Auxiliary Hospitals were set-up around Norfolk. Some of the county's mansions were used. Ketteringham Hall was not used as a hospital but to entertain convalescing casualties. Sir Maurice's sister had qualified as a doctor and was appointed Commander of the Auxiliary hospital at nearby Swainsthrorpe.

Modern Ketteringham is a member of the Swardeston group of parishes. The vicar of Swardeston in 1865 was the Rev. Frederick Cavell and his wife, Louisa gave birth to their daughter Edith. In 1895 Edith tended to her sick father and once he had recovered, she decided that her vocation was to be a nurse. She trained at the London Hospital. She spent some time in Brussels before the war and when the war started, she went there. When Brussels fell to the Germans she remained, tending to the wounded irrespective of nationality. She also helped British soldiers to escape to neutral territories. The Germans arrested and executed her, creating outrage back home. She became a heroine of the First World War and a statue of her was erected in Norwich.

At the now famous moment of the eleventh hour of the eleventh month of 1918 the guns fell silent as the armistice began. After the war, opposite the Village Hall, Sir Maurice carved out a small plot from the field edge and erected a monument. The monument is a Celtic wheel-head cross with the inscription:

> To the glory of God and a memorial to the part taken by Ketteringham in the Great War 1914-1919

Sir Maurice honoured the whole village for playing its part. It was villages, such as Ketteringham who produced the nation's food, kept 'the home fires burning' and maintained the morale of the troops.

Monument to the fallen in the Great War, Ketteringham, 2011.

The men of Ketteringham who died have another memorial on the north side of the nave of the church. Here the names of the seven men are recorded, Arthur George Beaumont, John William Betts, George Betts, Walter Henry Dawson, Cecil Humphreys, John Page, Reginald William Tooke. Listed not by rank or in chronological order of death, but alphabetically. There is no roll of honour which records all those who served. In such a small community the loss of seven men and an unknown numbered injured was felt by all.

Like any industry, agricultural profits are dependent on market price and, as was seen in the depression of the late 19th century, when prices fall there are serious implications for landowners. In 1920 agricultural prices began to fall as Britain again felt the effects of cheap imports. Wheat fetched an average of 18s 10d a cwt but three years later the price was 9s 10d a cwt a reduction of a half. During the previous recession, landowners had anticipated that the fall in prices would be temporary and, consequently, if they waited things would return but this time, they made no such assumptions. Despite improvements it had proved difficult to find good tenants for Tacolneston Hall. The fall in agricultural prices, and the inevitable fall in rent from the farms, resulted in Sir Maurice putting the Tacolneston Estate up for sale by auction in March 1920. The decision to do so must have required plenty of soul searching. This was where he, Margaret and his brother Raymond were born and raised. His title was Sir Maurice Boileau, 3rd Baronet of Tacolneston not Ketteringham. With the loss of this Estate and its 2,044 acres, the Boileaus would cease to be members of the greater gentry[12] and became lesser gentry or 'squirarchy'.

The sale particulars for Ketteringham which Sir John pondered over in 1837 (see p.81) and the ones for Tacolneston produced for his grandson in 1920 (see p.107), show how the English estate, or how England viewed their estates, had changed. Both were freehold Estates of over 2,000 acres. The Tacolneston Estate was described as "comprising virtually the whole of Tacolneston Village". The earlier Ketteringham Estate as "including nearly the entire parish" of Ketteringham[13]. Tacolneston Hall is described as a Queen Anne residence with 16 bedrooms, four reception rooms and two bathrooms. Ketteringham Hall was described as in the Elizabethan Style with 13 bedrooms, 4 reception rooms. Other than reference to Tacolneston having the modern features of electric lighting and two bathrooms the particulars would be very similar. However, Ketteringham was sold as a single lot with mansion and farms[14]. Tacolneston was sold in 97 lots. The economic viability of the English Estate made them difficult if not impossible to sell. Since 1910 there had been a growing demand for farms. Farming profits had been increasing since 1906 and had increased further during the Great War. This resulted in an increase in land value. Breaking up the estates and selling the Estate farms in separate lots was now the practice to receive an economic return. In 1837 there is a brief mention of the Estate farms "with convenient farming buildings and cottages for labourers". Eighty three years later Tacolneston refers to cottages which "are picturesque and suitable for conversion into Week-End Cottages". Both particulars mention the convenience of the location with regards to Norwich. Tacolneston has the addition it is only one mile from Forncett Station on the Great Eastern Line. The train has made the weekend cottage in Norfolk possible.

Both agents chose to market the properties as having good game. Whereas in Ketteringham Hall's particulars a small reference is made to, "Extensive woods, forming fine preserves for game," Tacolneston is described in bold as, "A residential, sporting and agricultural property," with sporting being placed before agriculture. The hunting season had become more profitable and such a property might now be bought as a place merely for the shooting.

The breaking up of Estates into small lots was widespread. The editor of Estate Gazette wrote in January, 1920 of the previous year's record year of sales, with the continued break up of innumerable ancestral domains, all England seemed to be

By direction of SIR MAURICE C. BOILEAU, Bart.

NORWICH

10 MILES FROM THE CATHEDRAL CITY.   3½ MILES FROM WYMONDHAM.
3 MILES FROM NEW BUCKENHAM.
1 MILE FROM FORNCETT STATION ON THE MAIN G.E.R.

IN 97 LOTS—FREEHOLD.

The Attractive and Valuable RESIDENTIAL, SPORTING & AGRICULTURAL PROPERTY

known as the

Tacolneston Estate

Situated in the Parishes of TACOLNESTON, FUNDENHALL, BUNWELL, FORNCETT ST. MARY and FORNCETT ST. PETER, extending to some

2,044 ACRES

and including (Lot 1) the well-known and Charming Moated

Queen Anne Residence

TACOLNESTON HALL

containing 16 Bed and Dressing Rooms, Two Bath Rooms, Four Reception Rooms and complete Offices, with ELECTRIC LIGHT fitted to every room; together with Stabling and Lodge, BEAUTIFUL GROUNDS and Woodlands, and GRANDLY TIMBERED PARK OF 100 ACRES, in all about 137 Acres, with Home Farm, other Farms and ample Cottages available.

16 Capital Mixed Farms

of from 47 Acres to 225 Acres.

NUMEROUS SMALL HOLDINGS of attractive and convenient sizes, with Houses and Buildings.
VALUABLE ACCOMMODATION LANDS.   MIXED WOODLANDS.

THE FULLY-LICENSED "PELICAN INN."

And in a number of Attractive Lots, several

CHOICE VILLAGE OCCUPATIONS AND 56 COTTAGES

many of which are picturesque and suitable for conversion into **Week-End Cottages,** mostly situated in and comprising virtually

THE WHOLE OF TACOLNESTON VILLAGE.

also the

LORDSHIP OF THE MANOR OF TACOLNESTONE AND WILLIAMS IN TACOLNESTONE.

Which will be offered by Auction (unless previously Sold), by Messrs.

JOHN D. WOOD & Co.

AT THE "ROYAL HOTEL," NORWICH,

On SATURDAY, 6th MARCH, 1920,

At 12.30 p.m.

Land Agent: E. W. BECK, Esq., 16, Bank Street, Norwich.
Solicitors: Messrs. JANSON, COBB, PEARSON & Co., 22, College Hill, London, E.C. 4.
Auctioneers' Offices: 6, MOUNT STREET, LONDON, W. 1.

Ward & Foxlow, Printers, Harcourt Street, London, W 1

Tacolneston sale, 1920.

changing hands, every county being represented in the great revival and in the stupendous transactions.[15]

Ketteringham Hall's neighbour, the East Carleton Estate was sold in lots by Mrs Steward seven months after the Tacolneston sale. The Ketteringham Estate however, remained as a Norfolk estate village. Like many estates the lord of the manor felt a certain control over the church serving his tenants. In Ketteringham, a closed village where all the parishioners were also tenants of the squire, this had resulted in disagreements as to who was ultimately in charge of spiritual matters. This occurred again in the inter-war period. When Mr Walker, of Ivy House Farm arrived in Ketteringham, at the end of the 19th century his mother approached Sir Francis about building a Methodist chapel in the village.[16] Sir Francis had not agreed to this request, so she started holding services in the farmhouse entrance and became part of the Attleborough group of churches or 'circuit' as they are known within the Methodist Church. When Arthur Walker married, his mother and father, moved to High Ash Farm and Arthur became church leader. The vicar, Gilbert Hart was not concerned about the new Christian gathering with parishioners attending both services. The kindly Rev. Gilbert Hart left and was replaced by the Rev. William Duxson who, knowing the beliefs of Lady Boileau, Sir Francis' widow, kept his services in the Low Church tradition. When Lady Boileau died in 1925, however, he reverted to his High Church preferences and filled St Peter's with candles, hung a crucifix from the beam and wore an assortment of vestments during the service. This was not well received by the parishioners but was encouraged by Ethel, Raymond's wife and, now having a choice of places to worship, many attended Ivy House Farm, although the Boileau and their servants still attended St Peter's. The number attending Ivy House became too great for the space available, so Sir Maurice was approached again. He was unable to remove the unpopular vicar but did offer a site for a new temporary building at a small rent. The vicar saw this as Sir Maurice's support for the nonconformists and although he was churchwarden, stopped him reading the lessons in church.

A small chapel was erected in Ketteringham in 1929 with the help of many in the village and Sunday school was held at High Ash Farm. The chapel was apparently well attended unlike the village church. The building was only temporary and the lease on the land was renewed annually. In 1943, with both Sir Maurice and his brother Raymond dead, the request to renew the lease was turned down which, it is believed, resulted in the chapel being dismantled and moved to Long Stratton where it was rebuilt.

In 1937 Sir Maurice had died and was buried, like his parents, aunts and sisters, in the churchyard rather than his grandfather's mausoleum. He had never married and had no heirs and the Ketteringham Estate passed to Raymond his brother, the only surviving child of Sir Francis. He succeeded to the title 4th Baronet Boileau, of Tacolneston Hall although he did not inherit Tacolneston Hall.

On the 3 September 1939 many of the villagers attended St Peter's Church, Ketteringham as normal. The daughter of the Estate's painter and decorator, Daphne Reeve, then ten years old, remembers leaving the village church and the chauffeur's ten years old son, George Evans running down the road to meet them shouting "We're at war!" He had heard, along with many of the people of Britain, the Prime minister announce that following Germany's invasion of Poland: "This country is at war with Germany". At the same time the National Service (Armed Forces Act) 1939 introduced conscription for all men between eighteen and forty-one. Yet again groups of young men from Ketteringham received their call up.

Following the experiences of the First World War plans had been prepared for potential future conflicts. One was the relocation of children from areas that might be targets of enemy bombing. These children were known as evacuees. Ketteringham was considered a suitable safe location for some of these evacuees. They were placed with families in the village. Nine arrived in Ketteringham to join the thirty-three children of the village. Sir Raymond's Estate Steward, Mr Hadingham took in some evacuees. His only daughter, Catherine spoke of how, as an only child, she enjoyed their company and made a lasting friend who would return to visit long after the war ended.

In June 1940 France surrendered and the Battle of Britain began. Norwich suffered its first air raid 9 July 1940. It destroyed the Boulton and Paul box-making and sheet-metal shops as well as the printing department, canteen and boardroom, killing twenty-six.

Anticipating the requirement for military airfields, land was requisitioned. In 1940 an area of Hethel and neighbouring Stanfield Hall were chosen with work starting the following year to construct a bomber-station with three hard runways, taxiways and dispersal sites. On 11 December 1941 Germany declared war on the United States and they in turn declared war on Germany. The Americans agreed that despite also being at war with Japan the first priority was to defeat Hitler in Europe. This resulted in an influx of American military personnel and hardware being stationed in Britain. The RAF bomber site at Hethel was adopted by the American 12th Army Air Force who moved there in 1942, before the base was fully finished. In September 1942 RAF Hethel became the home of USAF 320th Bombardment Group and became known as Station 114.

This was a large base with both 310th and 289th Bombardment Groups joining the 320th. There were around thirteen-hundred personnel stationed at Hethel. The arrival of so many foreign young men must have had an impact, and the noise of bombers must have

Defence post Ketteringham, 2013.

shattered the rural peace. The only building in Ketteringham associated with the base were a defence post on the north side of the runway. The lane that ran from Ketteringham to Potash Farm had to be closed to accommodate the runway. It was reopened in 1954 but closed again and re-routed by Lotus to skirt the runway and their test track, joining St Thomas' Lane further to the east. The footpath that runs from High Ash Road to St Thomas' Lane once continued along the old Potash Road.

In June 1942 Sir Raymond died and, as he had no children, the baronetcy passed to his first cousin Francis who lived in Australia. The Estate, however, went to a different, senior, branch of the family. Sir John Boileau's (who brought the Estate) father had an elder brother and his great, great, great, great, grandson Etienne Henry Tudor Boileau inherited The Ketteringham Estate. He was in the army and brought his wife, Rachael and children, Valerie, Angela and Raymond to live in a small part of Ketteringham Hall that formerly was the home of Sir Raymond.

Eighteen months later, in December 1943 Ketteringham Hall was requisitioned and became the headquarters of 8th USAAF. The family was told to move out, but Rachel Boileau refused and the family was allowed to stay in a small part of the building. The Hall was emptied of the Boileau's possessions and became known as Station 147. The ground floor became the Operations Section, War Room and Intelligence Section. A mezzanine floor was constructed in Sir John's banqueting hall. Here officers could view a large operations map. The Hall's first floor became offices for the senior ranks and the second floor their quarters. The Boileaus had the wing facing the lake. The Hall alone was not sufficient to accommodate all the requirements of the 8th USAAF Headquarters and, like the neighbouring Hethel base, a 'village' was constructed within the village. Approximately 700 people were based around the grounds. Such numbers required additional infrastructure and a water tower was built along with a sewage works for the Hall and camp. Huts and buildings were placed around the hall as living quarters, stores, mess halls and a small hospital. One of the huts became a small concert hall which became known as 'the Opry House'. Sheriff's Avenue was lined with nissen huts. Whereas Hethel was a bomber base and therefore male dominated Ketteringham's administrative role was less so, Raymond Strong recalls:

> In the summer of 1943 we received our first WAC's. We got about 150 ladies of all kinds of talent. We got stenographers, linotype operators, truck drivers, and many other things that we needed. Later, we got another shipment of ladies and at top strength we had almost three hundred. This made many things run a whole lot easier than before.

Ketteringham Hall was now a military building and liable to attack, made easier as the building was painted white. To help make it less conspicuous it was camouflaged with paint and old engine oil. To the Americans the Hall became known as 'the castle' and its lake 'the pond'.

Major Edwin Reed with his staff at the 2nd Air Division Headquarters, Ketteringham Hall.

The American base became a village within the village of Ketteringham with sentry box at each entrance. The Hethel base covered many acres and the Americans used bikes in order to get around. Ketteringham was much smaller and the Americans used their bikes, amongst other things, to go to the Green Dragon pub in Wymondham. George Evans, who lived on Church Road near the Hall spoke of how the Americans gave the children sweets. He would, "shine the boys shoes for candy". There is talk of a local girl having a child by an American.

On 8 May 1945, Ketteringham's church bells rang to celebrate VE day, Victory in Europe. The church memorial to those Ketteringham lost in the 1914-1918 war were joined by, Fredrick Charles Browne and Hugh Alfred Salter. Later a memorial to the American airmen who died was placed in Hethel churchyard.

The month the war finished in Europe, the American bombers left Hethel and it became No 12 Group of Fighter Command. Mustangs of 65 Squadron and 126 were stationed there. In March 1946 two Polish Mustang squadrons were based at Hethel for a brief period as decisions were made about what role the Polish service men might play, now their homeland was under Russian control. Later that year the Poles left and all flying from Hethel ceased. The site was under the control of the Ministry of Agriculture in 1950 but remained with the Ministry of Defence.

In 1947, 110 years after John Boileau bought the Ketteringham Estate, Major

Etienne Henry Tudor Boileau sold the Estate to the trustees of the Duke of Westminster and purchased Rampisham Manor in Dorset. Raymond, his son, was at boarding school unaware that his father had sold the Estate. When he heard he was very disappointed he would never inherit Ketteringham where he felt "hefted". The Boileaus had saved the bankrupt Ketteringham Estate and returned it to its former glory as a fine family seat, although none were born at the Hall. The first half of the 20th century had seen great changes in Ketteringham.

The importance of the aristocracy in England and the status that it confers on a family has played a major part in Ketteringham's history. In the 20th century, things began to change. The effect that the two World Wars had on society is a topic much too wide, and Ketteringham much too small, to justify greater consideration here. However, two people who visited Ketteringham during the Second World War do show a change in British society. In 1945 a court martial took place at Ketteringham Hall, to consider the case of an American bomber crew who due to bad weather and faulty navigation equipment had dropped bombs over Zurich in neutral Switzerland. The Court's President was Colonel Stewart, better remembered as James 'Jimmy' Stewart the Hollywood actor. One of those who had served at the Hall remembers James Cagney appearing twice at Ketteringham's 'Opry House'. The age of celebrity had existed since Roman times, but these men were not celebrated because they had won wars or came from an aristocratic families, they were 'merely' film stars.

The sale did not bring an end to the Ketteringham Estate. It had been purchased in its entirety as a working estate. Ketteringham Hall was part of the sale but what of its future in the post war age?

Notes

1. TNA RG13/1852.
2. NRO
3. NRO PD 42/11.
4. NRO, cutting dated 13 Nov 1912, p.1095.
5. Storey, *Norfolk in the Great War*, p.27.
6. Ibid., p.45-46.
7. Forces War Records.
8. Ibid.
9. Ibid.
10. Ibid.
11. Ibid.
12. Barnes, *Norfolk Landowners since 1880*, p.84.
13. Farebrother & Co, Wymondham Town Archive.
14. John D. Wood & Co, Wymondham Town Archive.
15. Ibid. 5, p.69.
16. NRO, *Journal of the Wesley Historical Society: East Anglia*, No 116, December 2013.

The Break-up of the Estate

The War brought much change to Ketteringham with the arrival of the evacuees and the Americans as well as the sad loss of life. It is not easy to detect whether the influx of new inhabitants and their different backgrounds had any effect on the villagers. Those who remember that time have said "didn't think about it. It was war time". The evacuees went back to their homes, the Americans to new bases. The aftermath of the war, however, continued to bring major changes to the village. The immediate post war housing shortage resulted in the accommodation left by the Americans being used by squatters before the local authority took it over to help meet the county's housing needs. Ketteringham already had a village store and a second store was added for the 'camp' as it was known. The additional population resulted in Ketteringham getting a bus service to Norwich, although it was possible to obtain all you needed in Ketteringham. Hall Farm, as well as supplying the Hall, sold milk and butter, the grocer, butcher and baker delivered from Hethersett and a man even came to the village with a horse and cart selling ice cream.[1] The Hall had a paraffin run electric generator which villagers used to charge their household accumulators (batteries). Ketteringham post war differed greatly from pre-war Ketteringham. It, like the country, had to come to terms with a world modernising at an ever-greater pace.

When Etienne Boileau put the Estate on the market in 1947/8 it was purchased by the trustees of the Duke of Westminster. Ketteringham Hall was no longer required as a home. In 1950 the Hall was let and became Ketteringham Hall Preparatory School school under the headmaster, Mr Giles. Catherine Hadingham, daughter of the gamekeeper, remembers one of the early actions of the new owners was to cut down the trees in Smeeth Wood. The value of timber had increased following the war and, like those who previously owned the Estate, was a useful source of income. Four new modern houses were built on High Street for Ivy House Farm. Mr Walker's comments on the lack of accommodation for his farm workers finally being addressed. The new owners were prepared to invest in the Estate anticipating any future financial returns coming from its agriculture and consequently maintained it as a working Estate. The war and its aftermath had shown the need for the country to produce as much food as possible. Although the Estate's income came largely from food production the financial benefits were not seen by the landowners. Rent controls, introduced during the war, continued resulting in greater prosperity for the farmers and not the landowners. With the increasing returns from agriculture and the greater prosperity of those who farmed the land it is not surprising that land prices rose. In 1945 land in Norfolk was £45 per acre but by 1949 it had risen to £76.[2] The owners of the estates not only had to deal with rents that did not keep up with inflation they were also hit by ever greater death duties resulting in many estates in Norfolk ceasing to be viable financially.

In 1951 the Oxburgh Hall estate was sold to a property company, Hunstanton Hall was sold the same year and became flats, the Dunston Hall estate was sold in 1957 and most of the Kimberly estate in 1958. Many country houses needed repair and modernisation and like Morton Hall, which dated back to 1599, were pulled down.[3] The demand for building land close to Norwich had started in the late 19th century and resulted in many estate owners selling land around the city. The Unthanks at nearby Intwood Hall made a good return on selling building land on the southern edge of Norwich.[4] However, Ketteringham Park was away from the population centres and could not help with these centres' ever-growing need for housing land. The Duke of Westminster's trustees appear to have seen the Ketteringham Estate investment as one in agricultural land and in 1958 with land prices around £100 per acre they considered the time was right to cash in their investment. The Estate was split into 79 lots and put up for auction with R.C. Knight & Sons with John D. Wood & Co the surveyors.

Near NORWICH, NORFOLK

Wymondham 2¼ miles   Norwich 5 miles   London 106 miles
Adjoining the main Norwich London Road (A.11)

The Ketteringham Estate

comprising

NINE EXCELLENT DAIRY AND ARABLE FARMS
with ample Cottages
TWO SMALLHOLDINGS   THIRTY-SIX COTTAGES
A FINE MANSION AND PARK

All let at low rents to first-class Tenants

Gross Rent £4,222 Per Annum

Tithe and Land Tax free

268 ACRES OF WOODLANDS AND PLANTATIONS

In all about

2,202 Acres

Forming Capital Investments

R. C. KNIGHT & SONS

WILL OFFER FOR SALE BY AUCTION IN 79 LOTS
(*except where sold privately meanwhile*)
On SATURDAY, 1st NOVEMBER, 1958, at 11 a.m.
At THE ROYAL HOTEL, NORWICH

Solicitors: Messrs. MILLS & REEVE, 74/75, Upper Close, Norwich (*Tel.:* 21587).
Surveyors: Messrs. JOHN D. WOOD & CO., 23, Berkeley Square, London, W.1 (*Tel.:* MAYfair 6341).
Auctioneers' Offices: 2, Upper King Street, Norwich (*Tel.:* 27161)
130, Mount Street, London, W.1 (*Tel.:* MAYfair 0023), and Branches.

Notice of Sale, 1958.

Comparisons have been made between the features selected by the agent for Sir Maurice's sale of Tacolneston Hall in 1920 and the particulars that Sir John perused in 1837. With the sale of the Estate in 1958 comparison can further be made between Tacolneston and the final sale of the Ketteringham Estate. The location is again featured at the top with both, in large letters, proclaiming the Estate's close proximity to Norwich. In 1920 the convenience of access to a railway station had become important; 38 years later the statement "Adjoining the main Norwich London Road (A11)", took its place, a reflection on the rise of the motor car. The distance to London has also become an important selling point worth mentioning. Under the Ketteringham Estate title the composition of the Estate is listed. It starts with the nine farms and their cottages then, two smallholdings, thirty-six cottages and last to be listed "a fine mansion and park". Ketteringham Hall now relegated to last on the list of the Estate's attributes. The market in the mid-20th century was for farms and farmland. The size of the Estate is given as 2,202 acres which is described as, "forming capital investments". Land is being sold as an investment. On the front of the sales document is stated, 268 acres of woodland and plantation. Whereas the sporting and hunting where considered the benefits of woodland at earlier sales, in 1958 it is described simply as woodland and plantation. The commercial value of timber had superseded that of leisure.

The auction took place at the Royal Hotel, Norwich on Saturday, 1 November 1958. Of the nine farms only three Ivy House, High Ash and Hall (Home) Farm were in Ketteringham. Station Farm is in Hethersett as are White House, Goward's and Planet Farm. Another White House Farm along with Wood House Farm are both in East Carlton. The tenant farmers made successful bids on their farms; Mr C. F. Harrison at High Ash and Hall Farm, Mr Cook at Ivy House. There were several pieces of Estate land rented by the tenant farmers who took the opportunity to consolidate these into their newly purchased farms. Messrs C. Cook at Station Farm in Hethersett extended his farm by purchasing the land he had previously rented on the Ketteringham side of the parish boundary. With the farms they purchased the farm cottages; Ivy House Farm five: High Ash: five, Hall Farm: one and Station Farm: two. Ketteringham Hall retained the Gardener's Cottage and Church Cottage but the other properties now became private dwellings. Thirty-six properties passed from Estate to private ownership. Those who had rented smaller pieces of land chose to purchase that land.

The impact of the break-up of the Estate was reduced by the ten years of ownership by the Duke of Westminster's trustees. Before their purchase at the centre was the Lord of the Manor and his family in their grand Hall. The trustees viewed the Estate as a business investment, the personal connection between village and Hall had gone. Those employed in service at the Hall had since found alternative employment. The village continued as a farming community.

Along with farming the other constant in Ketteringham's history is St Peter's.

Following the removal of the Methodist Chapel, St Peter's returned to being the sole building of worship in the village. When the Duke of Westminster's trustees bought the Estate the advowson remained with Etienne Boileau but in 1951 he transferred this to the Norwich Diocesan Board of Patronage. From 1939 to 1942 James McAnally, rector of Hethersett, served as vicar of Ketteringham. The Hethersett group of churches also included Great and Little Melton. Ketteringham remained part of this group to the mid-1980s when it became a member of the Swardeston group of churches. The former vicarage, Church Cottage, still belonged to the Hall. With the break-up St Peter's, the Estate village's church became the village church.

Even without the changes brought about by two World Wars the power of the Squire was gradually being eroded. Parish councils and District councils had been introduced under the Local Government Act of 1894. The local administrative role they performed was similar to the role the Squire had undertaken to ensure the smooth running of the Estate. It is, however, doubtful if many councillors would take it as far as Sir John Boileau and consider them to be that of 'father of the parish'. Ketteringham as a small community has a group parish council with neighbouring East Carlton.

The status of the farm owners was increased by the breakup of the Estate. The freehold of High Ash Farm was now with John Charles Foster Harrison who was also a member of the parish council and church warden at St Peter's. Consequently, he became a significant member of the community following the Estate's break-up.

At nearby Hethel airbase the squadron of Polish mustangs was disbanded in late 1946 with many of the Polish aircrews being absorbed into the RAF. Like Ketteringham the former huts and military buildings became post war re-homing although, by nature of its continued military use immediately after the war, this did not happen until 1950. Hethel Hall was by this time derelict and would be knocked down a few years later. The Hethel site was larger than Ketteringham boasting not only a general store and post office but a fish and chip shop, gym, chapel, cinema and social club. The chapel built by the Americans became the site's place of worship. The children on the site did not attend Ketteringham School but the nearer East Carlton or Bracken Ash. By 1951 the number of children on the site justified the opening of Hethel County Primary School. This was purpose built and described by Michael Coates, a former pupil, as being "superbly equipped". After eighteen months of opening the number of pupils attending was 120 and later reached 140, underlining the site's need for its own school. The school closed in the summer of 1958 as did the camp.

The Hethel site in the early 1950s was under the control of the Ministry of Agriculture but available to the RAF. In 1952 an American B-50 Superfortress took advantage of this. Running low on fuel it made a forced landing at Hethel in driving rain. It overshot the runway and landed in a ploughed field. In 1954 the future of Hethel was discussed. To accommodate modern aircraft the runway would need extending. The report read: "The extension of No. 1 runway [046/226 degrees] to the North-East would cut an unclassified road and a considerable proportion of Ketteringham Park would be taken up, many trees would have to be felled".[5] These are the trees of Inner Park Wood and the former deer park. This was an area carved out of the heavy lands that made up the former common. The report's closing comment that, "the site is said to be very wet,"[6] is therefore not surprising. Aerial photographs taken of Ketteringham Hall HQ by the Americans show these trees to have been cut down so it can be assumed that they had been replanted after the Americans left the Hall. A large part of the Hethel air base found a new purpose in 1966 when Lotus Cars moved into a purpose-built factory in which to build its sports cars. Potash Lane, which had been closed for the construction of the runway, was reopened in 1954 following its original route. It was again closed as part of the runway became a test track for Lotus Cars. Potash Lane was re-routed to follow the old perimeter track coming out near Ketteringham Hall's South (Ketteringham) Lodge. The footpath that runs from High Ash Road to St Thomas' Lane, where it joined the original Potash Lane, is still in existence. The section of the new Potash Lane that joined St Thomas' Lane was closed to traffic in 2005.

The country estate's struggle for survival in Norfolk was replicated throughout Britain in the 20th century. In Surrey, Fetcham Park,[7] the family home of the Hankey family since 1792, faced with the ever increasing demands of death duty, was put on the market by George Hankey. In 1920 most of the land was sold and in 1924 the house too. The house with 30 acres was purchased by the Rev. J.G. Wilkie as the new home of a boys' boarding school he was running from his rectory in Badingham, Suffolk. Following the death of both the Rev. J.G. Wilkie and his widow the house had to be sold to pay off the inheritors.[8] In 1965 an Educational Trust bought Ketteringham Hall and Badingham College relocated there. It was run by the son of Rev. J.G. Wilkie, the Rev. Alan Wilkie. The disused air raid shelters at the front of the Hall were knocked down and the lawn turned into a sports field with swimming pool. Church Cottage became the 'Master's Cottage'. The college did not last long and in July 1968 Ketteringham Hall was back on the market. John D Wood of London was again involved and the Royal Hotel, Norwich the same venue as that of the Tacolneston Estate and the Ketteringham Estate sales. The description of a "Country Mansion of Tudor Origin" still is a desirable description but

Badingham College dining room, 1965.

The College playing field and swimming pool.

where once the availability of land for sporting pursuits meant shooting game it now referred to sports fields for playing games.

The break-up of the Estate resulted in a change of ownership of both property and land. The Lord of the Manor which had become the institution at the centre of the Estate for hundreds of years was no more, but the village was still a community rooted in agriculture and farming. Much has been made in this book of the significance of the type of land and its soil on the village's development. It is therefore not surprising that in the sales details at the Estate's break-up the following appears:

> SOIL — The Estate is most favourably situated, being on the junction of light and heavy soil. For the most part it comprises medium deep loam, being heavier on the West and South and lighter on the North and East. The land is very suitable for dairy and corn growing.

Both Ivy House and High Ash Farm had cow sheds for around fifty head along with dairying facilities to suit, Hall Farm facilities could accommodate a more modest eight cows. The farms' milk went to supply the demand from the ever-growing population of Norwich.

The Lord of the Manor had always enjoyed hunting on his Estate. The villagers had, apart from when employed or required as helper and beaters, been excluded from this pursuit. Details of the sale included the remark, "the Sporting Rights over each Lot will be included in the sale". Sporting Rights in Ketteringham were no longer the preserve of those who lived at the Hall.

Apart from its church, Ketteringham had a general shop and post office and a bus service that ran on Wednesday, Friday and Saturday to Wymondham and Norwich. The blacksmith had gone but High Ash Farm had a small blacksmith's shop. Much had changed from the earlier part of the century. The sales particulars give details of each lot. Mains electricity was now supplied to all but two houses, Vernon Lodge and Smeeth Bungalow, the latter had its own generator. The water supply installed by the Americans, known as 'Estate Water', was supplied to nearly all houses via a standpipe but Vernon Lodge and Lone Cottage still used a well, Foldgate Cottages had a bore hole and the South Lodge 'Council Water'. Only the farmhouses had bathrooms.

Lotus Cars had been manufacturing their cars at Hethel since 1965 and in 1970 Colin Chapman, their founder, purchased Ketteringham Hall. In 1977 Colin moved his personal office from the car plant on the old Hethel air base to Ketteringham Hall to be closer to his racing team and away from the financial difficulties of the road cars. Ketteringham Hall was a useful, quiet, out of the way location, where innovative work could be carried out in secret, far away from the rest of the British motor racing teams centred in Oxfordshire. The location came with drawbacks. Ketteringham Hall was away from the ready supply of experienced staff who might have knowledge of developments happening in racing. The finances for a state-of-the-art racing team were not good at Ketteringham. The other competing formula one (F1) teams were building up their in-house capabilities but, 'Team' (as Team Lotus were known locally), struggled with this. The eight fabricators on site were reduced to four in 1978 as money became ever tighter.[9] This did not stop Team Lotus becoming F1 World Constructors' Champions that year. The stable block built by Sir Francis

Colin Chapman's office at Ketteringham Hall, photographed in 2004 just before being cleared.

Boileau, turned into classrooms by Badingham College, now became workshops. Suddenly Ketteringham was a centre for technological innovation something which would have sat well with Sir John Boileau.

Emerson Fittipaldi's Lotus 72/7 photographed outside Ketteringham Hall in 2006.
Fittipaldi raced the type 72 chassis number 7 in 19 Grand Prix, winning five of them. It was restored to its 1972 black & gold specification by Classic Team Lotus.

The village sign being unveiled, 1979.

Both the village shop and school leases expired in 1973 and, as was the case in many small villages, both closed.

The Boileaus of Ketteringham Hall were no longer at the centre of the village but the village hall they had built was. One of the village's groups that met there was the Women's Institute (WI). In 1978 the WI celebrated its Diamond Jubilee and groups throughout Norfolk organised the construction of new village signs for their communities to mark the anniversary. Under its chairwoman, Mrs M. Lamb, Ketteringham's branch decided to do likewise. As a small group with limited funds one of the members, Pauline Pleasants asked her husband Eric if he would be willing to make the sign. He was a talented wood carver and agreed to undertake the task. Eric and Pauline Pleasants lived in Ketteringham at the small North Lodge of Stanfield Hall.

Eric was an interesting man with a fascinating past which he recorded in a book, *Hitler's Bastard - Through Hell and Back in Nazi Germany and Stalin's Russia* by Eric Pleasants, edited by Ian Sayer and Douglas Botting. In the book he explains where he learnt his wood carving skills. He spent much of the war in occupied Europe. While on the run in occupied Paris he was captured and briefly became involved with the Waffen SS. When the war ended, he found himself on the Communist side of the Iron Curtain and was arrested by the KGB on charges of espionage and sentenced to twenty-five years hard labour. While imprisoned in one of Stalin's gulag he was involved in a fight during which Eric struck a man who fell, hitting his head on the frozen ground and died. In this brutal environment killing someone can give status to a prisoner and Eric was invited to join the Blatnoy, a form of Russian Mafia. On joining, his bed was moved near the stove, he was given blankets, food and a reduced workload. He found a piece of old hacksaw blade while working in the mine. This he sharpened and used it to shave. He started chipping away at pieces of wood. He carved a chess set and many years later the Ketteringham village sign.

Eric carved a man guiding a plough pulled by oxen, an apt way to represent Ketteringham's rural history. The village name is decorated with fruits of harvest. The post has the WI motif and the year 1979. The plinth is a carved piece of stone, from the old Sunday school with the Boileau's Pelican crest.

Two years earlier the nation had celebrated the Queen's Silver Jubilee and the village planted a tree and placed a seat at the junction of Church and High Ash Road. The tradition of celebrating royal events in Ketteringham seen with planting of a walnut tree by Lady Mary Heveningham at the restoration continued. When Eric Pleasant's sign fell down in 2011 a number of the villagers' considered a new sign to celebrate the Queen's Diamond Jubilee the following year.

Unlike many others the Ketteringham Estate had survived the mid-19th century depression in agriculture, the Great War and Second World War, but in the second half of the 20th century it was no longer. The village had experienced the transition from an Estate village dominated by Ketteringham Hall to a village little different, at first glance, from many other Norfolk villages. The village economy was a rural one before and after the break-up of the Estate. It is perhaps not surprising that the farms, when passed from the ownership of the Hall to the tenant farmers, would see few changes. The economic activity generated by the Hall had been reduced when the Hall was occupied in the Second World War by the Americans and, after the war, the general economy of the country had shifted away from domestic service. Ketteringham's location, close to Norwich and Wymondham and the Lotus Cars design and manufacturing plant, would result in employment being available with only a modest commute. However, with an estate village past stretching back hundreds of years, Ketteringham could not be separated from its heritage. Ingrained in the village, it could not be forgotten despite all traces being lost in only a few decades.

The Estate had passed from the old established Heveningham family to a family who had made their name as lawyers, a professional group of people; it was then owned by a merchant followed by a family of a clothier; not forgetting an actress. The estate had passed from established families to the professional classes. This in many ways reflected English society. The change to the background of the new owners was only possible by a change to the process of transfer, the Estate had become a commodity bought and sold. Once purchased the importance of transfer by marriage and inheritance remained as before. The purchase of an Estate was more than a means to buy a nice home with land that could provide income, it was a means of entering the landed gentry and the status and standing that gave in English society.

Ketteringham's church gives evidence to this in the memorials erected by new owners. The memorials honour past family members who never lived at the Hall or ever visited the church, but their mention gives the impression that this had been the family seat for generations. The Estate gave a man the opportunity to stand for parliament. Whereas Arthur Heveningham may have turned in his grave at a lawyer being Lord of 'his' Manor perhaps his grandson William might have appreciated that the Estate gave Nathaniel Peach the opportunity to stand for East Norfolk.

The Ketteringham Estate had provided status but it, like other estates, was a business and a business needs to produce more than status to survive. The former Estate farms are, like Ketteringham Hall, independent business all with a shared history.

Notes

1. Coates, *Memories of a Hethel Childhood 1950 to 1955*.
2. Barnes, *Norfolk Landowners since 1880*, p.79.
3. Ibid., p.31.
4. Ibid., p.63.
5. Delve, *The Military Airfield of Britain: East Anglia*, p.102.
6. Ibid.
7. Historic England, IOE01/08071/18.
8. Wikipedia.
9. Lugvigsen, *Colin Chapman inside the innovator*, p.302.

Ketteringham's New Road

In the autumn of 1987, the residents of Ketteringham awoke to the sound of the newly opened , Wymondham and Hethersett bypass. The new concrete road surface, yet to be smoothed by traffic, produced a tyre noise which travelled easily, unimpeded by the newly planted trees too young to provide any sound screening. In the damp air, the roar shattered the peace that had existed for centuries. Residents had warned the planners that the junction with Station Lane, which required motorists to cross first one of the dual carriageways then wait in the central reservation before crossing the other carriageway, would be dangerous. The warnings were well founded. Many improvements have made to this junction during the following twenty-five years. In the meantime, traffic found that a safer and more pleasant route for all, apart from Ketteringham's residents, was to go through the village and cross the A11 via the bridge on Ketteringham Lane. This increase in traffic and the ever-present traffic noise were the more obvious effects of the new A11, but from a historical perspective the road changed far more.

The stream of flowing traffic on a modern dual carriageway has a similar impact on the landscape as the flowing water of a river. Both are routes for trade and communication. They act as a barrier which can only be crossed at a certain safe point and create convenient territorial boundaries.

The A11 formed a barrier for 6 km between Cringleford and Wymondham which could only be crossed at one point, Ketteringham Lane. Ketteringham lost its foot path that once joined it with Hethersett and the road connection from Five Ways to Hethersett. Hethersett lost its connection to Hethersett Station although this was not as serious as it might have been if the station had not closed in 1966. The new road faced opposition as it cut through former Sillfield Common and considerations had to be made for a colony of great crested newts who inhabited the ponds on the common's wet land. The road also cut through part of Smeeth Wood as it followed the course of the railway line but, whereas crossings were placed on the rail track for the paths connecting the Squire's farms, there was little to justify a new bridge across the new

Aerial photograph taken in 2011 showing how the A11 cut Station Lane in half. This photograph shows the improvement when it no longer became possible to cross the dual carriageways at Station Lane.

road here. The ancient Anglo-Saxon ties with its former great estate centre were limited to the single connection along Ketteringham Lane and the old paths to the Great Common were lost.

Roads, and to a lesser extent rail routes, now form the basis of the nation's internal trade network. The A11 linking the regional capital with the nation's capital provides an important route for trade and communication. Ketteringham's position on a major trade route did not result in it becoming a location for commerce but one for the maintenance of the route. South-Norfolk chose the junction of Station Lane with the A11 as the site for its highways department. A company who specialises in highways works located in the same area. A recycling centre was placed close to the A11 junction allowing waste to be transferred by heavy lorries straight onto the adjacent road.

The stream that flowed between Ketteringham and East Carlton had formed the boundary between two groups as the land was first divided up, this eventually became the parish boundary which runs just to the south. The new flowing A11 separated the parish land on the southeast edge of Hethersett from the main parish and, similarly, the parish lands on the edge of Cringleford were cut off from their parish by the A11/A47. These 'territories' were transferred to the civil parish of Ketteringham.

The land included the medieval manor of Cantelose. The Domesday Survey records Hethersett as having two churches, one was to become Hethersett's parish church St Remigius, the other was at Cantelose and became All Saints. The latter was united with Hethersett's main church in 1397.[1] As this was only 48 years after the Black Death, Cantelose has been described as one of the plague's deserted villages. Whereas the plague played its part it was not the cause of the manor disappearing. Domesday records St Remigius as having 60 acres and a value of 5s. Cantelose's church by contrast had a mere 8 acres and a value of 8d. This suggests a very poor living and with a loss of many of the clergy during the plague it failed to attract a priest. The inhabitants who survived the plague likely relocated taking advantage of the shortage of labour in other locations. All Saints served as a free chapel before being demolished at the time of the Reformation. The church exists today as a few stones in a field north of Cantley Lane. Although the boundary change moved Cantelose and other areas to the civil parish of Ketteringham the ecclesiastical boundary remained unchanged.

The old parish boundary between Hethersett and Ketteringham, which once wove from one side of the railway line as it followed the edge of Medieval fields was redrawn to run down the centre of the new A11. The disused Hethersett Station became part of Ketteringham.

The new road changed Ketteringham. The arrival of roads/tracks or ways in the past had resulted in, or resulted from, great change. The descendant of hunter gathers who made the spring their home had seen the arrival of the track that connected the two water crossing points at Intwood and Wymondham and the tumuli that marked its route.[2] Boudica's rebellion brought a Roman road connecting the Roman town of Venta Icenorum with Denver and beyond. The desire to create a private estate by the Atkyns caused the closure of the ways that would had been in use since Medieval times had required the construction of a new road that followed the perimeter of the estate. This road, Station Lane and East Carleton Road, is an early 'bypass' and now possibly the busiest road in the village.

Roads and tracks evolved as Ketteringham evolved. Their arrival and disappearance are evidence of changing requirements, an indication of village life and culture at different times. They help to tell the history of Ketteringham's evolution as an estate village. Roads and tracks are ubiquitous features in many different landscapes and cannot therefore be seen as uniquely creating estate villages; the reason I have chosen to base this chapter on the arrival of a new road is twofold: the route physically separated the village from much of its past and it was the first major change that happened to Ketteringham since the estate was broken up. Both provide a suitable opportunity to consider the village now in the early 21st century and what part the legacy of its estate past still plays in the village today.

The book's opening chapter took one of the most important events in British history, the regicide, to consider the part Sir William Heveningham played in it but more importantly why he was able to participate. That was possible because Ketteringham Hall provided a family seat grand enough to support a suitable standing in society. Having started with Ketteringham Hall it is appropriate to return to the Hall today.

Even before the Estate's break-up in 1958, Ketteringham Hall had ceased to be a family home, becoming first a preparatory school then a college. In 1970, it was purchased by the founder of Lotus Cars, Colin Chapman. In December 1982 Colin Chapman died of a massive heart attack. Team Lotus never regained their glory days after the loss of their founder and in 1995 work stopped on the development of a new F1 car (Lotus 112) and the staff at the Hall were laid off. Group Lotus continued to lease Ketteringham Hall from the Chapman family using it as a conference centre.

In 1996 the Malaysian car manufacturer Proton Cars purchased an 80% holding in Group Lotus International Ltd, which increased to 100% in 2003. Proton Cars were established from a desire of the then Prime Minister of Malaysia, Tun Dr Mahathir bin Mohamad, to create a national car industry. When the Malaysian Prime Mister visited the United Kingdom at the start of the 21st century, he took the opportunity to visit 'his' company's acquisition at Ketteringham Hall. The Hall relived some of its past glory as a ministerial cavalcade drove through its gates and the Hall, once again, hosted a dinner for a visiting dignitary. When Group Lotus's lease expired, Ketteringham Hall was converted into individual offices for rent, a purpose it still fulfils to this day. The great depression of the late 19th century had caused many of the estates of England, whose income was generated by agriculture to cease to be economically viable. The depression was, in part, caused by technological advances in transport which made it possible to import cheap food from around the globe. Transport technology played a part in the decline and loss of some country houses, however, Ketteringham Hall's involvement in transport technology may have been responsible for saving it.

The Boileaus have now long departed from Ketteringham Hall but one organisation, formed by Sir Raymond in 1901, continues, the Ketteringham cricket club. When Ketteringham Hall became a school the parkland became a sports grounds with a pavilion. Ketteringham Hall cricket club still play on the Hall's ground and uses the cricket pavilion. When Group Lotus held the lease for the Hall the employees formed an angling club which fished the top lake next to the Hall. This continued as The Ketteringham Hall Angling club after Lotus left the Hall. The club closed on 31 January 2015 due to falling membership.

St Peter's church still stands in the shadow of the Hall reminding all of the historic links both share, entwined with their estate heritage. Its interior displays

The cricket pavilion—legacy of the Sir Raymond's love of cricket, 2006.

the memorials to the families who once lived next door. Past connections between church and Hall are obvious to resident and visitor alike. Others are not. Since medieval times St Peter's has owned glebe land in the village. As with other land, since the end of open field farming individual strips had been exchanged, combined and enclosed, these enclosures had seen further exchange resulting in the glebe forming two large enclosures (fields) by the latter half of the twentieth century. In 1978 all glebe land became the ownership of the Diocesan of Finance and the rent for the land allocated to the Diocesan Stipends Fund for the payment of clergy stipends. In 1984 the glebe land was again exchanged for a field in a different location in the village.

Richard Haggar would no doubt be relieved that the disagreement as to whether St Peter's should be a catholic or protestant place of worship had been settled for some time. It is an Anglian place of worship, belonging to the diocese of Norwich, and still provides for the pastoral needs of the village. Ketteringham is no longer part of the Hethersett group of parishes but now resides with the Swardeston Group. This could be seen as another move that separated it from its ancient Anglo-Saxon connection with its former Great Estate centre of Hethersett, alternatively, a reconnection with its former medieval hundred of Swardeston. A more prosaic but likely reason is it is no more than an example of the modern Anglian Church coming to terms with having too many small rural village churches in sparsely populated parishes.

Church attendance is less now than it was, but the church still plays its part in the community, it runs events in the village such as coffee mornings, a Lent lunch held at the village hall and, in addition to the harvest festival service, an annual harvest supper. The bells are still rung at weddings and other important occasions as they have since 1420 when Henry Grey had the first bell hung; later joined by a second in 1490 then further added to by Sir Arthur Heveningham. St Peter's bells are enjoyed by many visiting groups of bell ringers, Ketteringham having some of the earliest bells that can be rung full circle.[3] The crypt, blocked up by Sir John remains blocked enclosing Sir William Heveningham's remains. The boxed pews built for the Squire's family and servant, remain. One is now used as an ideal location for the young children of the village to play and remain safe during services, a much safer location than the balcony built for the children of the village by Sir John Boileau. The balcony can still be used as additional seating when the church is full or for those who wish to have a bird's eye view at a special service. The Boileau mausoleum in the churchyard is a reminder of Sir John's ill-judged idea to make room in the crypt for his wife's passing.

The monuments in the church tell the story of Ketteringham's estate village past. When it ceased to be an estate village its history did not end and evidence of post-estate times can be found in the church. On the altar are two candlestick holders that once belonged to Badingham College and were donated to the church when the college closed. The lynch gate was built in memory of Commander Kite, the former principal of the preparatory school. The organ was restored in 1991 with the assistance of donations from former members of the HQ Staff who had been stationed at Ketteringham Hall between 1943-1945. Although no longer the estate church of an estate village, St Peter's is still a recorder of the village's history in a tangible way.

The former estate farms remain. High Ash Farm is still run by the family of Mr Harrison, the tenant farmer who purchased it in 1958. The economics of modern farming had meant that dairy farming no longer takes place in the village, but cattle have not disappeared completely from the landscape. A piece of land in Ketteringham

The lynch gate, 2004.

is designated as a county wildlife site and here Highland cattle graze. This ancient breed can feed on uncultivated vegetation and are well suited to maintaining undergrowth. The breed is not too dissimilar from cattle that were once kept in the village and grazed the common. Sheep have returned and are now a familiar sight in the village fields, a reminder of those recorded nearly one thousand years ago in the Domesday survey. Sugar beet, first tried by Mr Walker in the early part of the 20th century, is still grown in the early the 21st. The village's connection with the area's agricultural community is still strong. Ketteringham Smallholding is the location for Wymondham Countrysiders and Young Farmers annual rounders match and barbeque.

In 1912 Arthur Walker of Ivy House Farm had been asked by a journalist as he passed by the farm cottages, if they were sufficient for all the labourers. "No" was the reply; "there is some difficulty in providing houses for all who require them". One hundred years later the number of people employed on the land has decreased as farms have become more mechanised and use is made of contract workers. At the start of 2014 Brian Hall left his tied cottage where he had lived having worked for Ivy House Farm. His departure meant that, apart from the farm manager at High Ash Farm, there were no farm employees resident in Ketteringham. Although the first time since before feudal times, that does not mean present day Ketteringham is void of those who work the land. Some residents use their land for equine purposes and manage the land accordingly. Others have small holdings selling produce from the roadside and many more just grow vegetables for their own use. The connection with the land is not lost. The old farm cottages now make attractive rental properties for professional workers employed outside the village. The houses on the south side of High Street have large front gardens to make use of the southern growing area and as new houses were built planning regulations required that they conformed to the existing building line retaining the large front gardens at the expense of a smaller rear garden.

People have always used local materials to construct dwellings known as vernacular buildings. They have cut timber in nearby woods and made thatch from reeds growing by streams. Near the many buildings constructed from clay-lump is invariably a pond formed when the clay was dug. In more recent times sand and gravel have been required to construct not only houses but roads. When the glaciers of the Anglian Ice Age melted, they left large deposits of both sand and gravel. This was first quarried locally to fulfil local requirements. The 20th century not only increased the need for these materials but provided the means to transport such heavy bulky materials to more distant locations. Some of the farmland to the east of the parish has been quarried to extract these materials, then used as landfill sites before being backfilled with topsoil and reverted to agricultural land. The eastern end of Ketteringham Park became a site for gravel extraction but was then filled with commercial waste before being covered with topsoil. This has not been returned to agriculture but given to the community and is now under the ownership of East Carlton and Ketteringham Parish Council. In addition to what was once Ketteringham Quarry the former boundary of Ketteringham Park is also included. This is known as Ladybelt and the site is appropriately called Ladybelt Country Park. Within the park is the icehouse of Ketteringham Hall which apart from providing a place of historic interest, is a bat hibernaculum.

As an estate village any development in Ketteringham was agreed with the Lord of the Manor in order to maintain its character to his liking. The number of houses reflected the needs of the estate's farms and Hall. Current development in the village must be agreed with South Norfolk Council planning department. When South Norfolk Council consulted on possible land for development to ease Norfolk's housing shortage Ketteringham was considered. A defined development boundary was drawn around much of the existing built on land in which development might be considered although stating: Very little infill can occur without affecting the form or character of the village. The report went on to state: "The setting of the village in open countryside is made apparent by the significant breaks in the built-up area to the north of The Street around the war memorial and between 'Cytringa' and 'Thatched Cottage' to the South of Low Street. These afford views over the surrounding countryside".[4] The village's rural character, valued in the 19th century is still considered important in the 21st.

Development has taken place. The small plots of land bordering High and Low Street, purchased at the break-up have largely been built on. Ketteringham now has a village garage, Ketteringham Motor Services (now NMG Motor Engineers) opened in 1984, very close to where the former blacksmith had his workshop and repaired horse drawn wagons and farm machinery.

The village school has long gone but there is a nursery school near the church. Ketteringham Hall is now the location of a number of companies and organisations. The South Norfolk Highways Department is still located next to the A11 junctions along with a recycling centre and several other companies.

Since the 'new' A11 was opened Ketteringham has experienced many more cars. Some use Ketteringham Lane to cross the 'new' road, others Station Lane to avoid the busy Thickthorn junction where the A11 meets the A47. To those passing through in a car the wealth of history and interest features of the village may not be obvious. Some visitors choose to visit Ketteringham's Ladybelt Country Park, where it is possible to see the icehouse, lower lake and gain an impression on how the park once looked. There is a tearoom in the orangery of Ketteringham Hall where one can sit on the terrace and sense the former grandeur of Ketteringham Hall. Both offer a glimpse of the history of the Hall at the centre of the estate. For those with more time, the estate village and its history can best be appreciated from a walk through Ketteringham.

Notes

1. Norfolk Explorer, NHER No9469.
2. Sharpe, *The Journal of the Open University History Society*.
3. Cattermole, *Church bells and bellringing: A Norfolk Profile*.
4. South Norfolk, Site specific allocations and policies document.

Ketteringham's Estate Heritage

Much is written about the life of those who dwelt in the country houses at the centre of various estate villages. Equally much has been written about the lives of those who were employed in these houses, gardens and those who worked on the estates' farms. Justifiably so, as these English estates are a microcosm of English society and its class system. This is a subject that holds fascination beyond these shores and therefore, with the added backdrop of a fine house and countryside, lends itself to many a period television drama.

Ketteringham Hall was never the grandest of country houses. The sale particulars of 1837 under the description of Capital Mansion added "of moderate size". Those who called it their family seat were never, despite trying, in the top tier of aristocracy. It is unsurprising that little has been written about Ketteringham and when it does get a mention it is invariably as a backdrop to another subject such as Team Lotus or Second World War airfields.

I hope I have shown that Ketteringham has a fascinating history which for its size is remarkable. Ketteringham does not offer the guided tour of the grand house, the chance to see opulent rooms laid out as they had been two hundred years before. It does not offer the opportunity to make comparisons between the life of those downstairs with those upstairs and wander in gardens with manicured lawn bordered by weed free beds. Ketteringham does not promote any particular period and if it did it would likely be the present. It is, on the surface, a typical modern Norfolk village. One does not, however, need to delve far below the surface to see its estate village past. This is not surprising when considering apart from the last sixty or so years it was such. Remaining as an estate village into relatively recent times is fortunate for those who wish to appreciate the village's estate history. As estate village it was a farming community and, following the break-up, it remained as such. The village farms have no requirement for a pool of local labour and with most inhabitants employed outside the village it cannot now be described as such. However, the rural setting of the former estate houses largely remains, the small infill of housing an indication of the village adaption to its post-estate future.

The relatively unspoilt nature of the village means it can be appreciated by pleasant walks or by car with many convenient places to pull over. Either way the lack of a wider familiarity with the village's history offers the opportunity to appreciate these without the crowds often experienced elsewhere. This chapter is a guide for those who might choose to explore and discover Ketteringham's past first hand.

Entering Ketteringham from the A11 or East Carleton one arrives at Five Ways. Standing here and looking to the east it is possible to see some of Norwich's larger buildings such as County Hall and the castle. It also provides the opportunity to gain an appreciation for the wider landscape in which Ketteringham sits. Ketteringham is on higher land on the edge of Norfolk's central clay plateau which runs from the northwest Norfolk coast down to Suffolk, formed of boulder clay left over from the Ice Age. The Rivers Yare and Wensum have their source on the plateau. Both flow to the lower ground to form a great estuary from which they join the North Sea.

While at Five Ways it would be hard not to notice two large mounds of earth. *(see map on p.135 number 1)*. These are Bronze Age burial mounds dating back 4000 years, not surprisingly, the oldest structures in Ketteringham. The larger of the two is twenty-five metres in diameter and two metres high. Originally it was surrounded by a six-metre-wide ditch. A part of the ditch is still visible on the west side.[1] The second mound is slightly smaller, being sixteen metres in diameter, it too was once surrounded by a ditch.[2] These are scheduled monuments and should not be walked upon. The tools used to build these were little more than antlers and wicker baskets. The mounds may well have been the resting place of important people. Their purpose was, however, to do more than honour the individuals. These were substantial construction in a prominent position intended to make a statement in the landscape which was, "this is our land, this is the land of our ancestors". Their impressive location on top of the ridge caused David Gurney, Norfolk's County Archaeologist, to describe them as some of the finest in the county. To those who only know this junction by car it appears a four-way crossroads, there is however, a bridleway which begins here and is the fifth way. In medieval times, and long after, the route of the bridleway was the Highway to Intwood. *(see map on p.135 number 2)*. If one walks down the track and looks back and imagines the mounds when first built it is not hard to appreciate the statement they would have made. Further along the track curves as if going round an imaginary object. Here was once another burial mound that has disappeared under the modern plough. It too once marked out the land of the ancestors. The track has been used since prehistoric times being part of a network which connected the lower estuary with the higher plateau lands.[3] The section of the track from the lost mound to Five Way became part of a Roman road that connected the Roman town of Venta Icenorum, 6 km to the east, with Denver and the Fens. Ketteringham High Street for its first mile from this junction also follows the old Roman Road.

The road going east from Five Ways is Cantley Lane, once known as the Highway to Norwich. It continued to Cringleford where a ford/bridge crossed the Yare and then on to Norwich. When the new A11 was built it was diverted to join Thickthorn roundabout. The main road through this junction is the road constructed following an agreement between Sir Thomas Beevor and Edward Atkyns to bypass Ketteringham Park in 1789 *(see map on p.135 number 3)* (chapter 6). It also led to

Hethersett Station which Sir John Boileau had built in 1845 (chapter 7).

The land around the junction is divided into several large arable modern fields.[4] The size of these fields may be considered by some as the less desirable feature of modern farming which does not represent the traditional patchwork of the English landscape. Their size, however, is still small compared to the great open medieval field that once existed here. It was Carleton Field, one of the three that were part of Ketteringham's open field farming discussed in chapter 2. The area to the south of the track was known, in Medieval times, as Twydale, the two dales.[5] Although less open now it does give an opportunity to gain a feel for Ketteringham during the period of open field farming. A reminder that Ketteringham has been a community based on farming for hundreds of years and that changes in farming practice are not new.

Ketteringham's estate village heritage is apparent the Victorian gothic Norwich Lodge which once provided the grand entrance to Ketteringham Park. (see map on p.135 number 4) From here a drive ran through the park taking in the best views of the lakes and icehouse framed by the tree belt before sweeping round to the front of Hall. On the lodge are displayed the coats of arms of Sir John Boileau. Whilst one walks around the village it is interesting to note whose coat of arms appears on different building. An indication as to whom the initiated the building work. (see Appendix 3).

Opposite, in the centre of the junction, is the obelisk that Sir Francis Boileau commissioned in celebration of the 60th year of Queen Victoria's reign in 1897 (see map on p.135 number 5)(chapter 7). The connection between the landed gentry and the aristocracy is an important one to the estate village. The head of the aristocracy being the monarch it is not surprising that this monument exists. Opposite the mounds that honour a former headman, on a Roman Road built after the defeat of a tribal leader, Boudica, a monument is placed in honour of the nation's head. It would be wrong to assume the choice of location has any underlying meaning in relation to these earlier features but it does reflect the prominence of the ridge as a visual setting. In 2005, on the bicentenary of Norfolk's famous son Nelson's victory at Trafalgar, it was planned to use this location to light a beacon as part of the commemoration.

Travelling along High Street the first six hundred metres follow the route of the Roman road. Although initially built for largely military reasons following the Boudica rebellion, the new road connected the first- century community with the wider trading network of Roman roads. To the north of High Street the A11 is both visible and audible connecting twenty-first century Ketteringham with the modern road network.

The fields on the northern side of High Street would once have formed Hethersett field, another one of the three large medieval fields. Hethersett's St

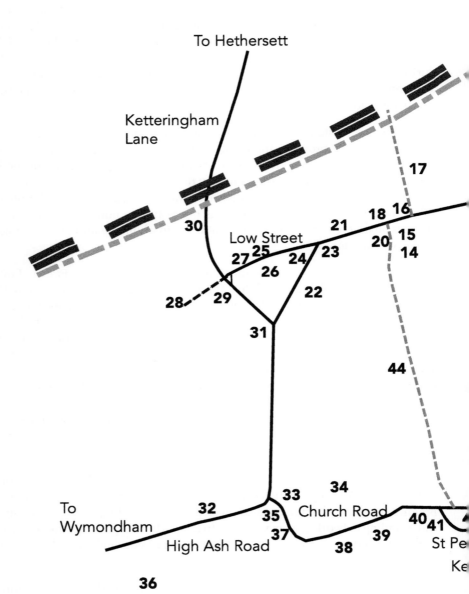

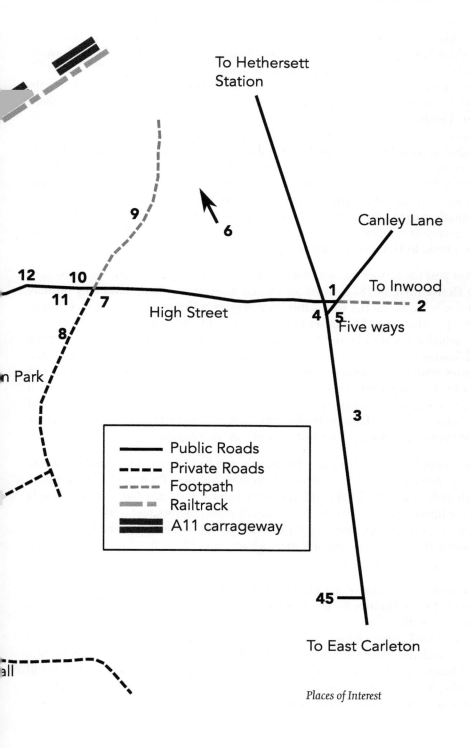

To Hethersett Station

Canley Lane

To Inwood

High Street

Five ways

n Park

To East Carleton

Places of Interest

Public Roads
Private Roads
Footpath
Railtrack
A11 carrageway

Remigius church is visible beyond the A11 *(see map on p.135 number 6)* close to it would once have stood an Anglo Saxon Hall, the centre for the Hundred, of which Kitrincham belonged. The first building on High Street, after Norwich Lodge, is Station Lodge (now called the Lodge), *(see map on p.135 number 7)* modernised in the late twentieth century when the original fell into disrepair. High Street has two of the five lodges that once provided access to Ketteringham Park. Unlike Norwich Lodge it does not display a coat of arms to the Lord of The Manor, however, the current owner, Colin Dalton has carved two pelicans, the symbol of Sir John Boileau and placed them on the neighbouring gate posts. The posts are either side of the private road, Ketteringham Park[6] *(see map on p.135 number 8)* but was, in Medieval times known as Over Gate Waye. The term gate is, like dale, from the Danish meaning way. On the other side of High Street is a footpath marking the continuing course of the old way *(see map on p.135 number 9)* curving as it follows the plough practice of the medieval ox plough. This path was a route to Hethersett Station.

Just past the former way are two semi-detached cottages built for the workers of Ivy House Farm in 1878, when Sir Francis Boileau was Squire and they proudly display his crest on the west gable. *(see map on p.135 number 10)* At Ivy House Farm *(see map on p.135 number 11)* the soil starts to become heavier as light loam is gradually replaced by the heavier clay. Here the road leaves the course of the old Roman road with a slight southerly bend. The next two sets of semi-detached houses were estate houses built by the Duke of Westminster, *(see map on p.135 number 12)* built around seventy years after the previous cottages. They are much larger reflecting changing expectations in accommodation. Whereas Sir John and Sir Francis Boileau chose to display their coat of arms on their buildings the Duke of Westminster's houses have just a simple 'W' monogram.

An example of an earlier pair of estate cottage, Appletree Cottage and the White House *(see map on p.135 number 13)* are next but one. Built in the 18th century, both make use of the local building material and are constructed, not surprisingly on the heavier land, of clay lump. On the other side of the street is the 17th century, Juniper Cottage, *(see map on p.135 number 14)* a farmhouse built when the Heveningham's were Lords of Ketteringham, possibly in the days of Sir William Heveningham (chapter 4).

In front of the house stands Ketteringham Village Hall. *(see map on p.135 number 15)* Sir Maurice Boileau's initials are displayed on the outer west wall. This was given to the villagers as a place where they could gather as a community when the men left Ketteringham to fight in the Great War. In 1919 a further piece of land was provided opposite on which the War Memorial was erected dedicated to, "the part Ketteringham played in the Great War" *(see map on p.135 number 16)*. It still stands proud in its rural setting, surrounded by the former estate fields where the men once worked. The Service of Remembrance takes place at the church, but it is a village tradition that a child from the village places the wreath at this Memorial in remembrance of the role of the villagers in times of conflict. A loke runs along the east side of the field where the memorial stands. *(see map on p.135 number 17)* Two hundred metres along the loke is the railway bridge that Sir John had built to allow cattle to cross from one part of the estate to the other. The War Memorial and village hall became the centre of the village and the bungalow next to the hall was formerly the village store.

On the same side as the War Memorial is a semi-detached house. It has been suggested that this was once *The Bull*, the village public house *(see map on p.135 number 18)*. I have found no historic evidence of this and Sir John would not have allowed a pub on his estate. From its proximity close to the village hall and shop, it is easy to see how it lends itself to that story.

From, the village hall continuing west there is a footpath on the left *(see map on p.135 number 19)*. This leads to the village Church of St Peter's and Ketteringham Hall. For those wanting a shorter walk to visit these fine buildings this is an option but to appreciate the full history of the village I recommend continuing along High Street and saving this path for the return journey.

The next building on one's left is the former school and schoolhouse *(see map on p.135 number 20)*. Sir John paid for a new school building and teacher. It opened on 28 January 1840 remaining in use until the 1970s.

On the right are two semi-detached cottages that bear their estate village heritage with the initials, MGB 1934 *(see map on p.135 number 21)*. Beyond these High Street bends as it meets Low Street. It is not difficult to make the correct assumption that Low Street was formally the continuation of High Street. In 1827 Nathaniel Peach had the bend constructed to cut the corner to High Ash Road *(see map on p.135 number 22)* from his desire to make Ketteringham Park private (chapter 6). Just before this junction, set back from the road, is Eric Pleasants's village sign *(see map on p.135 number 23)*. The carved scene that once graced the top is now in safe storage having deteriorated after many years of exposure to the weather (chapter 9).

The new route of High Street created by Nathanial Peach's cutting the corner resulted in the former section of High Street becoming the modern Low Street (chapter 6). Low Street led to the common and is the area where the village migrated to be close to the common edge (chapter 2). At the start of Low Street, on the left is a 16th century Thatched Cottage *(see map on p.135 number 24)*. Between this and the

Sheep grazing opposite Wellgate Cottages, 2014.

old smith's house, is a small holding. Although only a recent addition to the village it resembles, in both size and location, the small holding that appears on the sales particulars of the estate Sir John Boileau bought in 1837. When the sheep are put on this land for summer grazing it is possible to imagine earlier times. Opposite the field are Wellgate Cottages, the oldest dwellings in the village *(see map on p.135 number 25)*. The cottages take their name from the Well at the gate designed by Sir John Boileau's architect, Jeckell. On the side facing the road Sir John's crest is displayed to passing road users. The smith's forge became part of the garage for one of the newer properties built in the 1960s. The smithy's house became the post office *(see map on p.135 number 26)*. Once the forge would have kept the village's rural economy running by repairing farm machinery. Nearly opposite the old smithy is the modern equivalent NMG Motor Engineers keeping the villagers' and surrounding area's cars running. *(see map on p.135 number 27)*.

The end of Low Street forms a T-junction with Ketteringham Lane. This was once a crossroads, the track opposite was an ancient drift way that led to the common *(see map on p.135 number 28)*. Now it is a private farm track with no public right of way. Just before the junction is a narrow left turning which is the continuation of Low Street. This forms a small triangle of land in the centre of which stands a well *(see map on p.135 number 29)*. This junction is the end of the original High Street. A road that starts at its east end with Bronze Age burial mounds and ends in the west with the former Medieval common, in parts a Roman Road, a Saxon track and a Viking Gata.

At the T-junction to the right is one of the former farms on the common edge. It is now known as Bridge Cottage *(see map on p.135 number 30)* due to its proximity to the bridge built in 1846 to cross the new railway line. If ever there is a group of people gathered on the bridge I recommend asking what might be coming down the line. It is not unusual for a steam locomotive to be using this track and the bridge is an ideal viewing point. Watching trains from the bridge has always been a popular pastime. This is where the blacksmith's son took it a bit far in 1852 and was arrested for throwing stones at a passing train. The bridge is now joined by a second bridge to allow users of the lane to pass over the A11. This lane leads to Hethersett which was once Ketteringham's important Anglo-Saxon centre now Ketteringham's important local centre supplying both schools, shops and pubs. The lane crosses the course of the old Roman Road running from Five Ways just the other side of the bridge.

Bridge Cottage and common, 2013.

Turning left at the T-junction one re-joins Low Street. The picturesque, thatched cottage on the left is Avon Cottage *(see map on p.135 number 31)*. It faces the heavy clay lands as it has done for five hundred years. Look out over the open arable fields and it is not difficult to imagine this as the vast Medieval common it once was (chapter 4). Standing water can often be seen in the field, prevented from draining away by the heavy clay. The sixty-acre wood known as Smeeth Wood (known locally as the Smee) sits beyond the fields. One of the few pieces of ancient woodland remaining in Norfolk. If lucky it is possible to see herds of both Roe and Red deer who have lived here for thousands of years, particularly conspicuous in the rutting season and winter.

Just past Avon Cottage, Low Street re-joins High Street at the end of Nathanial Peach's corner cut. Although it came into being in 1827 it is a relatively new junction. In medieval times Ketteringham Lane would have continued through the woods opposite (New School Wood) to the church. It was, not surprisingly, known then as Church Waye. There is a guidepost at the present junction. The road to Wymondham is straight as it travels across the former common. The common was enclosed as families combined their medieval strips of land on what was the third great field known as Ketteringham Field. Walking down this road the view to the right offers further opportunity to appreciate the size of the common in earlier times. The house in the foreground is Lodge Farm *(see map on p.135 number 32)*. Like the other estate buildings it displays a Boileau coat of arms, in this case that of Sir Maurice Boileau. If one turns to look back at Avon Cottage and Bridge House, it can be appreciated how they hug the former common edge.

The road is straight typical of one built across a former common or by a Lord of the Manor, who as the owner of the estate could place a road wherever he chose. In the time of the Atkyns, the road had a curve to the east. The old course of the road is still visible in the woods next to the road. The junction to Church Road is the point where High Street ends and becomes High Ash Road. The building here is Wymondham Lodge *(see map on p.135 number 33)*.

Wymondham Lodge has recently been enlarged. The modern extension is joined to the older building by a passageway enabling one to appreciate how the lodge once looked. This lodge appears on the sales details in 1837 as the lodge to Church Road. Sir John Boileau had a new entrance drive built to the Hall. Behind the lodge the tree lined avenue, known as Sheriff's Avenue, can clearly been seen *(see map on p.135 number 34)*. Named in honour of Sir John becoming Sheriff of Norwich in 1844. For the new entrance avenue to provide maximum grandeur the route of High Ash Road was moved slightly north.

Bridge and Avon Cottage on common edge, 2015.

This brought it in line with the new Sheriff's Avenue. Oak trees were planted along the verge of High Ash Road to give the impression it was all part of the entrance drive. He referred to this section of High Ash Road as the Avenue.

At the lodge is Church Road. High Ash Road (The Avenue) continues to Wymondham. Here there is a convenient bench to sit and decide which one to explore. The bench commemorates the Queen's Silver Jubilee in 1977 *(see map on p.135 number 35)*. At the start of High Street is a monument to Queen Victoria so it is fitting that at the end of High Street there is another one to Queen Elizabeth II, her great-great granddaughter.

With the straight road ahead, the large open fields and Smeeth Wood to the right it is possible to appreciate the size of the former common. There is a footpath 300m on the south side which joins St Thomas' Lane *(see map on p.135 number 36)*. If taken, this can form a circuit as St Thomas' Lane joins High Ash Road further along its route.

High Ash Road takes its name from Sir William Heveningham's messuage that became High Ash Farmhouse and is the road the messenger rode with the news of Sir William Heveningham's death at the start of the book. Running along the side of both the latter part of High Street and High Ash Road are drainage ditches. Their depth gives an indication of how wet this land is. Past the High Ash

High Ash Farm House, 2013.

Farmhouse St Thomas' Lane meets High Ash Road. This is the parish boundary were Ketteringham meets Wymondham.[7] Here the straight road curves as the former Ketteringham common meets Wymondham common. When Ketteringham common ceased to be, High Ash Road came into being as a direct route but only up to the parish boundary. The other side of the road was Wymondham common and remained as such until 1810. This has resulted in a kink as High Ash Road joined a new when Wymondham common was enclosed (chapter 6). At this junction High Ash Road becomes Browick Road. The thatched cottage at the junction is called Foldgate. A gate once existed at the end of High Ash Road so livestock could be grazed on the wide verges either side of High Ash Road.

If one decides to make a circuit and travel along St Thomas' Lane to return along the footpath there are other points of interest. The first is the name, St Thomas' Lane. From the time of the Heveningham's this was known as Sir Thomas Beevor's Lane after Sir Thomas Beevor of Hethel Hall (chapter 6). The road follows the parish boundary as far as Clapslough Farm.[8] At this point the parish boundary turns perpendicular to the south. Further along St Thomas' Lane, just past a small lodge, it re-joins the lane at a perpendicular. The unusual route of Ketteringham's parish boundary is a result of Anglo-Saxon manors and their complex landholdings. This was part of a manor once owned by the Saxon thane Ulf and became part the lands of Stanfield Hall. The small lodge is the North Lodge of Stanfield Hall. In the sixteenth century Henry Heveningham purchased part of it, the rest remained with Stanfield Hall. The boundary runs through Stanfield Hall. The Hall cannot be seen from Ketteringham. It can be seen at a distance from the north side of the B1135. Further along St Thomas' Lane one cannot fail to miss the aircraft hangar. Behind is the Lotus test track built on the old World War Two Hethel air base. The hangar was not part of the original air base.

If a walking circuit has been decided upon then the footpath that returns one to High Ash Road is just past the cottage opposite the hangar. This footpath is a continuation of the original route of Potash Lane. The original route can still be seen opposite. When the test track was built Potash Lane was moved to follow the runway perimeter road. This now joins St Thomas' Lane a short distance further along, but this has since been closed to traffic and can only be used by cyclists or pedestrians.

Returning along High Ash Road to Church Road the woods on the right (see map on p.135 number 37) were the former site of the quarters for the women serving at Ketteringham Hall when it was the HQ of the US 8th Bomber Group. To the left is an excellent view of Sheriff's Avenue (see map on p.135 number 34). This was also lined with Nissan huts during the war. Church Road became the preferred entrance drive to the Hall for Sir Francis and the old grand drive built by Sir John ceased to be used long before the Americans arrived. The houses on Church Road (see map on p.135 number 38) are more evidence of Ketteringham's estate heritage, each set of houses proudly display they were built for Sir Maurice Boileau in 1913. They were built for those who worked at the hall. Next are the former barns, milking sheds and cart sheds, now converted into dwellings, which were built for the modernisation of Hall Farm, also known as Home Farm (see map on p.135 number 39). The farmhouse, and former rectory, is next (see map on p.135 number 40).

At its end Church Road is forked. In the centre is a grass triangle in which stands a guidepost indicating Church or Hall (see map on p.135 number 41).[9] Either way you pass the old Sunday School (now called the estate house) built by 1898 by Sir Francis. His coat of arms can just be made out on the building's side. I recommend taking the turning to the church. Orchard Nursery is on the right and an orchard sits between it and the churchyard. The earliest glebe terrier at the Norfolk Records Office is from 1613. This records the vicarage as having one and a half acres with an orchard. To the left is the old vicarage now called Church Cottages (see map on p.135 number 42). This was the vicarage of the Rev. Robert Pecket. He was the vicar who would have given comfort to the Lady Mary Heveningham on receiving news of her husband, Sir William's death. He would have entered St Peter's church by a door at the east end, as the vicar still does.

From the start of the book I have made much about Ketteringham's historic charm and character deriving from its estate village heritage. In the five and a quarter centuries covered by this book, and in the many centuries before, St Peter's church has been at the centre of the village. A place where the village gathered for worship. Had their children baptised. Got married and said goodbye to their dead. This was their village church. The families living at the Hall adorned it with memorials to their families. They treated it as their private chapel. A village church or private chapel? It is probably both. St Peter's church was described by the author and Oxford historian Owen Chadwick as "a microcosm of the history of England".[10] Part of that history is the English estate village and this estate church tells it well. Consequently, I could have dedicated the entire chapter to the church and likely not have done it justice. This will only be a brief outline of what it has to offer the visitor.

Before discussing the points of interest the interior has to offer it is worth pointing out one usual feature of St Peter's exterior. It has a square western tower. In Norfolk, while there are one hundred and twenty-three round towers with an additional twenty-one ruined or lost ones, dating from the 11th and 12th century St Peter's is one of only six square west towers that exist.[11] One of the other five is nearby Hethel church which make these two the only square towers local to each other in the entire county of Norfolk.[12] The reason for such a prevalence of round towers in Norfolk is believed to be the strong connections with Germany in the Middle Ages and the resulting cultural legacy. The reasons why Ketteringham's is square, is not known.

On entering the church through the north porch a fine medieval font greets one. The coat of arms at its base displays the connections with the Hall and dates back to when the Hall belonged to the Greys with the Arms of the Greys and Redishams on the base. There are still signs, although hard to spot, of the bright colourful paint which survived the Reformation. In July 1608 the steeple fell and the parish register records: "the whole foot of the font was removed". The damage is still evident (chapter 4). As in many churches one is drawn down the aisle by the light of the east window with its fine stain glass. The window was a replacement for the previous 13th century one which, along with a new roof, was commissioned by Henry and Emma Grey. This patronage is displayed in the stained glass. In the main panel Sir Henry Grey is depicted in full armour. At the top of the panels four shields display his ancestry including that of John De Mowbray, the second Duke, who died in 1432. He was the nephew of Sir Henry's mother and this may have been a memorial to him in 1435.

There is a row of figures without heads. These are the saints whose heads were removed at the Reformation. In chapter 5, I considered the Reformation through the eyes of Ketteringham's priest the Rev. Richard Haggar. I hope I showed the massive impact this event had on the ordinary people of Ketteringham. When looking at the headless figures it is a chance to reflect that this was more than an act of vandalism.

Just beyond the fine pulpit is where the rood screen once was and one leaves the nave and enters the chancel. Under the east window is the altar behind which is a reredos. This is a late 16th century Flemish painting of the Marriage Feast at Cana. It is possible that Charlotte Atkyns brought this back with her from Flanders. The chancel was chosen by the Lords of the Manor to place memorials to members of their families.

On the south side of the chancel is a large chest tomb to Sir Thomas Heveningham, 1499. The first of the Heveninghams to own the Hall. In the north-east corner of the chancel there is a memorial to Lady Mary Heveningham and Sir William although he is not named because of his role in the regicide. Mary Heveningham's wish to be buried in the church was honoured. Under the brick and pamment floor is a burial vault. It may have had steps down to it under the altar but no evidence of an entrance to the vault remains. Blomefield records that Mary and William are buried in the vault. The 'traitor' William's coffin was placed here but it was broken up and his skull placed on Mary's coffin.

On the south wall, next to the tomb of Sir Thomas, the first Heveningham to own the Hall, is a large memorial to Edward Atkyns who bought the Ketteringham Estate in 1717 from Henry Heron and Abigail. The start of the inscription reads, "To the memory of Sit Edward Atkyns, one of the Barons of the Exchequer in the reign of King Charles the First and Second". As a judge at Sir William Heveningham's trial for regicide both had faced each other across a courtroom. Their memorials have for three hundred years faced each other across St Peter's chancel and will, no doubt, do so for many years to come. The Atkyns' monument is a copy of the one in the South transept of Westminster Abbey (chapter 6). Near the Atkyns' monument is a monumental brass to Lady Jane Grey. Her husband, Sir Henry Grey's brass has disappeared. There is also a brass to Richard Wright vicar at Ketteringham (chapter 5). On the north side is the plaque to Charlotte Atkyns with mention of her friendship with Marie Antoinette and Charlotte's attempts to rescue the Dauphin of France (chapter 6).

Return back down the aisle and it would be difficult not to notice that, like their predecessors, the Boileaus saw this church as their chapel and were happy to make it known. A gallery proclaiming that it was "Erected 26 September 1841 by Sir John P Boileau Bart" dominates the view. At the front (east end) of the church the box pews, where those who dwelt at the hall once sat, still remain as does the box pew opposite which the servants occupied. The position closest, to the altar, reminds all of the importance and standing of those at the Hall, separated from the villagers by the vicar's pulpit.

Where possible I have tried to give a feeling of the village beyond those who owned the Hall. This was not always easy but society began to change in the 19th century and ordinary people began to be recognised. This can be seen in memorials on the north side of the nave to cherished servants. One reads: "Mr. G Roles servant of the Boileau family, 1840, the monument erected by his employer".

Further down the aisle, on the south wall, is one of the larger wall mounted monuments to be found in the church. This is not for a former Lord of the Manor or family but a former vicar and his family, The Rev. Wayte Andrew. He was vicar of St Peter's from 1835 to 1887. During the 52 years he spent in Ketteringham he kept a journal. The Squire, Sir John Boileau was also keeping a journal at this time which enabled Owen Chadwick to write his book, *Victorian Miniature*, in which he brings to life the friction between the Hall's Squire and the clergyman. Behind the font is a door to the belfry. The public are not permitted to enter, but it is worth mentioning the bells that hang here. The oldest bell is from 1420 when the Greys were patrons. Another two were given by Arthur Heveningham in 1610 (chapter 10), after the tower fell in 1608. If one is lucky your visit might coincide with that of visiting bell ringers so they can be appreciated as they have for six hundred years. Next to the belfry door are the stairs to the gallery installed at Sir John's instruction. From the gallery it is possible to have a fine view down the nave to the chancel which was designed for the children and is both steep and narrow and requires great care. The church organ is located on the gallery, next to it is a brass plate in recognition of donations made by former USAF personnel for its restoration. To the right on the door is the memorial for the fallen of the two World Wars. They lived and worked on the estate and are given the honour of their names being recorded in the estate church. This may not be the largest or most grand of the memorials but it is the more important to the villagers who gather on Remembrance Day as the wreath of poppies is hung at its foot.

Should the autumn sky be clear the sun's rays will fall on the reredos behind the altar during the service. The ray of light falling on the painting as one of mankind's darkest period is remembered is particular to St Peter's due to its alignment. Churches are aligned east-west. In November the sun is due south at the meridian so sunlight entering through the windows on the south side should not touch the east wall. The reason the congregation at St Peter's can see the reredos illuminated is because of the building is aligned northeast-southwest. Some churches are aligned to the sunrise of the patron saint, but this would not account for the amount St Peter's deviates from the norm. It has been suggested that there is a connection with the pre-historic co-axial field system of Ketteringham which the church appears to follow.[13]

The walk down the aisle of St Peter's records the history of Ketteringham the estate village. Towards the door on the north wall is a plaque to John Charles Foster Harrison and his wife Norah. They were tenant farmers who bought their farm when the estate was broken up. It might be argued that their memorial in St Peter's is the transition from estate church to village church.

In the churchyard is the Boileau mausoleum built for Sir John and his wife following a controversial opening of the church vault (chapter 7). In front are the gravestones of later Boileaus who preferred not to be interned in the mausoleum. From the churchyard it is possible to see the thirteenth century nave's north doorway. The jambs of this doorway still display mass dials. These are small sun dials which, in the time before clocks, indicated the time of mass. There is a hole in which a stick can be placed to act as a gnomon.

In the churchyard, along with a row of head tombstones to servants who worked for the Boileaus at the Hall, there are plenty of more recent memorials to all who lived in the village. The church is still a place to remember and honour individuals who lived in Ketteringham.

Upon leaving the churchyard to the right, on the east side of the churchyard, are several parking spaces allocated for church visitors. From this parking area it is possible to see, although not enter, the stable yard built in 1899 for Sir Francis Boileau. Ketteringham Hall is a business premises and therefore the public are not permitted to enter the building or wander the grounds. The exception is the Hall's orangery. This has become the Orangery Tea Rooms. Whilst sitting on the terrace and enjoying the view of the lake it is easy to imagine the Heveninghams sitting there enjoying the deer park, the Atkyns enjoying the formal oblong lakes set in their park closed to villagers, or the Boileaus with the new Hall and grand gardens and the more naturalistic lakes we see now.

Leaving the Hall, you pass between two gate piers. These were erected by Sir Francis. One has the initials of his wife LHB Lucy Henrietta Boileau,[14] the other FGMB are his.[15] Just past the old Sunday School there is a footpath on the right which leads into a dark atmospheric yew wood. The path crosses the former winding entrance drive to the hall from Wymondham Lodge. It was given its current concrete surface by the Americans when stationed at the Hall. The path leaves the wood and crosses an arable field. To the left, the former water tower built to supply the USAF personnel, can be seen. (see map on p.135 number 44) Enter the next field, dog owners should be aware, is often used as sheep pasture. It provides a fine view of the back of Ketteringham's old school and the 17th century Juniper Cottage. The path becomes a short loke that meets the High Street with the village Hall to the right.

Much of Ketteringham's history is of either a direct, or indirect, result of the Ice Age. It was the anglian glacification 40,000 years ago that produced the boulder clay plateau which provided the perfect location for the tumuli and heavy land which became the common. It also left gravel deposits, which have been quarried to provide local building materials, over the centuries. In the twentieth century they were quarried on a larger commercial scale. Ketteringham had a quarry which, on closure was turned into a public park; now called Ladybelt Country Park. (see map on p.135 number 45) This is situated on East Carleton Lane which runs from Five Ways to East Carleton. Its entrance just past the 'dip' where the stream flows forming the ancient boundary between Ketteringham and East Carleton, in the woods on the right. The site is approximately 56 acres and an ideal place to walk. The park offering fine views of Ketteringham Hall and church across the former park lands. Here it is also possible to visit the icehouse built by Sir John Boileau to supply ice to the Hall and the aggrandisement of the park. The icehouse is now home to several bats. The park offering the opportunity to see other wildlife in well laid out woodland walks with many notice boards informing the visitor what they might see. The open park also affords the opportunity to appreciate different bird species and other wildlife.

Walk around Ketteringham and here its many historic buildings and sites are testimony to its past. The village history is recorded in its buildings but written by those who live in them. That village history will continue to be written.

Notes

1. NHER 9481
2. Ibid.
3. Sharpe, *Open University Historical Journal.*
4. In previous chapters I have used the terminology of the time I was writing about. Now referring to the modern landscape I assume the modern definition of a field.
5. Dale was a legacy of the Danelaw
6. Ketteringham Park is the official name for the road crossing the Park. It is sometimes referred to as Church Road which it joins.

7. The civic parish was moved in1987 to include Fold Gate Cottage.
8. Old maps call it Gap Slough. Slough means soil possible ref to Common.
9. Historic England listing 1050549.
10. Chadwick, *Victorian Miniature*, p.34.
11. Wade-Martins ed., *Historical Atlas of Norfolk*, p.56.
12. Ibid.
13. Ibid. 3.
14. Ibid. 9, listing 1050551.
15. Ibid. 9, listing 1170070.

Appendix 1—Holders of the Ketteringham Hall Estate

Thomas Heveningham and Ann	1496-1499
Sir John Heveningham and Alice	1499-1536
Sir Anthony Heveningham and Catherine then Mary	1536-1557
Henry Heveningham and Anne then Anne	1557-1574
Sir Arthur Heveningham and Mary	1574-1630
Sir John Heveningham and Catherine then Bridget	1630-1633
Sir William Heveningham and Catherine then Lady Mary	1633-1677
Lady Mary Heveningham	1677-1696
Henry Heron and Abigail Heveningham	1696-1717
Edward Atkyns	1717-1750
Edward Atkyns	1750-1765
Edward Atkyns and Charlotte	1765-1797
Charlotte Atkyns	1797-1824
Mary Atkyns	
Nathaniel Peach and Harriot	1824-1835
William Peach	1835-1837
Sir John Boileau and Catherine	1837-1869
Sir Francis Boileau and Lucy	1869-1900
Sir Maurice Boileau	1900-1937
Sir Raymond Boileau and Ethel	1937-1942
Major Etienne Boileau and Rachel	1942-1947
Duke of Westminster Trustees	1948-1958

Appendix 2—Vicars of the Church of St Peter, Ketteringham

1490	Richard Bocher	1761	William Wright
1490	John Cook removed	1786	Robert Burt
	Richard Bocher restored	1786	Mile Beevor
1501	Henry Smithson	1835	William Wayte Andrew
1515	Richard Wright	1887	Frederick Charles Dacies
1520	Henry Haggar	1893	Edmund Nelson Goddard
1530	Richard Haggar		Williams
1562	John Dixy	1899	Thomas Cutler Des Barres
1568	Adan Each	1905	John Still
1576	Henry Webb	1914	Richard Gilbert Keppel Hart
1584	Robert Grey	1925	William Edward Duxson
1591	Robert Jackler	1930	Jame Mortimer la F McAnally
1602	Richard Parker	1942	Harold Mundy Mills
1611	Richard Johnson	1955	Raymond Garth Heawood
1650	Miles Smith	1959	Douglas John Turner
1652	Robert Pecket	1966	Leslie Raymond Kingbury
1697	Richard Clark	1973	Michael Bowers Sexton
1707	Nathaniel Salter	1984	Philip McFadyen
1716	Thomas Tunstall	1991	Gordon Michael Campbell
1728	Samuel Clarke		Jones
		1996	David Jonathon Chamberlin
		2005	Paul Burr

Appendix 3—Insignia and Coats of Arms on Buildings

Lodge Farm House has Sir Maurice Boileau's Coat of Arms.

Boileau Crest (Pelican) and Coat of Arms, Norwich Lodge.

Boileau Coat of Arms, Well at Wellgate.

MGB (Maurice Boileau initials) and Boileau Coat of Arms, Village hall.

W (Duke of Westminster) initial.

what remains of the Heveningham Coat of Arms, High Ash Farm.

MGB (Maurice Boileau initials) with Boileau Pelican Crest, dated 1913, Church Road.

The Boileau family had two insignia:

1. Coat of Arms—Azure a Castle triple-towered Or masoned Sable in base a Crescent of the second
2. Crest—A Pelican in her piety charged on the breast with a Saltire couped Gules.

Index